The Divine Mystery.

The Gods, Known in Early Ages as the Incubi and Succubi, Now Known as the Elementals. Solving the Mystery of the Immaculate Conception and How it Was, and Is, Possible. Giving Full Instructions for Development, and How to Come Into Touch With the Elementals. Also

The Human Soul Before and After Death.

Constitution of Man and the Universe. Key of Gospels. Gospel Initiation. According to Pistis Sophia.

THE INNER MYSTERY.

By Dr. R. Swinburne Clymer.

The Mystery Solved.

GODS.

"THE sons of God saw the daughters of men that they were fair; and they took them wives of all which they choose."—Genesis 7, v. 2.

"There were giants in the earth in those days; and also after that, when the sons of God came in unto the daughters of men, and they bare children to them, the same became mighty men which were of old, men of renown."—Genesis 5, v. 4.

Beloved Scholar, the Mystery of the Ages has been the birth of the Christ. The Church has taught that Christ was of Immaculate Conception; but, believe me, that same Church has NOT believed in that Doctrine. It belongs to the men of that oldest and most mighty Fraternity to enlighten you and those who would listen, for we hold the secret, and we will give you it.

Does it seem so very strange that Mary might have conceived without human agency? It may seem strange to those who know not the secret, but surely the student can guess the secret, for it has been hinted at in all Rosicrucian literature.

In explaining this mystery to you, we do not intend to depend upon our explanation, but we will depend entirely upon the Bible, that book accepted as truth by all Christians, and we will also place before you the writings of the Holy Fathers.

In the Rosicrucian romance of the "Comte de Gabalis," or "Conversations Upon the Secret Sciences," by the Abbe

THE DIVINE MYSTERY.

de Villars, we read:

"When you shall be enrolled among the children of the Philosophers you will discover that the elements are inhabited by very holy creatures, whom, in consequence of the sin of unhappy Adam, his too unhappy prosterity have been forbidden to see or know. The immense space that is between earth and heaven possesses inhabitants much more noble than the birds and gnats merely; the vast ocean has many more dwellers than the dolphins and the whales; the depths of the earth are not created only for the moles; and the elements of fire, more noble than the other three, were not made to remain void.

"The air is full of an innumerable multitude of creatures of the human form; great lovers of the sciences, subtle, benevolent to the wise, but enemies to the stupid and ignorant. Their wives and their daughers are of bold and masculine beauty, such as painters have represented the Amazons.

"Know also that the seas and rivers are as fully inhabited as the air; the wise ancients have mentioned these populations under the names of Undines or Nymphs. There are few males among them, but a vast number of females; their beauty is extreme, and the daughters of men are not to be compared to them.

"The earth is filled to the center by Gnomes, a people of small stature*, guardians of the treasures of the mines and quarries; they are ingenious, friends of mankind, and easy to command; they furnish the children of the wise with all the money that they require, and ask little for their

---

*See the book, "The Irreconcilable Gnomes, or Continuation to the Comte de Gabalis," published by this house.

service, except the glory of being commanded. The Gnomides, their wives, are small but very agreeable, and their custom is very curious.

As regards the Salamanders, inhabitants of the region of fire, they serve the philosophers, but they do not wish to seek their company with much eagerness, and their wives and daughters rarely allow themselves to be seen; the wives of the Salamanders are beautiful, in fact more beautiful than all the others, because they are of a purer element. I pass over the description of these people because, when one of us, you will see them yourself at leasure, and easily if you have the curiosity. You will see their customs, their mode of living, their manners, their policy, their admirable laws; you will be charmed with the beauty of their minds, even more than with their bodies; but you will not be able to refrain from pity when they tell you that their souls are mortal, that they have no hope of the eternal enjoyment of divine felicity in the presence of that Supreme Being whom they know and WHOM THEY RELIGIOUSLY ADORE. They will tell you, that being composed of the purest particles of the elements which they inhabit, and having no contrary qualities in them, as they are made of but one element they do not die till after many centuries. But what is time compared to eternity? They return at last into eternal nothingness; and this thought so afflicts them that the philosophers have much trouble in consoling them.

Beloved Student, you will see that, although these Elementals are of the purest of the pure, they are not immortal, because they are ONLY of ONE element instead of a combination of the four. BEAR IN MIND THIS GREAT LAW. These Elementals CAN become immortal if some mortal will have intercourse with them. This is the great law. Bear in mind further, that there are but few males, and these males will seek intercourse with earth woman —as Genesis states, with the daughters of man,—

THE DIVINE MYSTERY.

(bear this in mind) IF THEY CAN FIND ONE MYSTICALLY INCLINED AND WHO IS PURE. So, as the Bible teaches, the sons of God see that the daughters of man are fair and they beget children with them.

"Now, bear in mind further. Unlike man, but LIKE Gods, these Elementals are TRUE TO ONE ONLY; thus it happens that, there being but few males among them, seldom will such an Elemental have intercourse with woman, and when they do a Christ or Saviour is born; for KNOW: "When the sons of God came unto the daughters of men, and they bare children to them, the same BECAME MIGHTY MEN WHICH WERE OF OLD, MEN OF RENOWN."

The student will now grasp the meaning of this mighty mystery, and will no longer condemn the mystery of the immaculate conception.

St. Luke 1, 26. And in the sixth month the angel Gabriel was sent from God unto a city in Galilee named Nazareth.

27. To a virgin espoused to a man whose name was Joseph, of the house of David; and the virgin's name was Mary.

28. And the angel came in to her, and said, Hail thou that art highly favored, the Lord is with thee, blessed art thou among women.

29. And when she saw him, she was troubled at his saying, and cast in her mind what manner of salutation this should be.

30. And the angel said unto her, Fear not, Mary, for thou hast found favor with God.

31. And, behold, thou shalt conceive in thy womb, and bring forth a son, and shalt call his name Jesus.

32. He shall be great, and shalt be called the son of the Highest; and the Lord God shall give unto him the throne of his father David,

THE DIVINE MYSTERY.

33. And he shall reign over the house of Jacob for ever; and of his kingdom there shall be no end.

34. Then said Mary unto the angel, How shall this be, seeing that I know not A MAN?

Our student must note this question carefully, for she asks the direct question: "How shall this be, SEEING I KNOW NOT A MAN?

Answer: "And the angel answered and said unto her, the Holy Ghost shall come upon thee, and the power of the Highest shall overshadow thee; therefore also that holy thing that shall be born of thee shall be called the son of God. (The son of a God.)

Always bear in mind that the words Holy Ghost means nothing short of the word "Fire." Holy Ghost is the Spirit, and in its final essence Spirit is the Fire. So the overshadowing of Mary was nothing other than that of a son of God, the Elemental of Fire—a Salamander.

Now, note further what the Abbe de Villars had to say:

"Our fathers, being TRUE philosophers, and speaking to God face to face, complained to him of the wretched fate of these people; and God, whose mercy is illimitable, remembered him that it was not impossible to find a remedy for this evil."

He made known to them that in the same manner as man, by the alliance which he has contracted with God, has been made a participator of the divinity; so the Sylphs, the Gnomes, the Nymphs, and the Salamanders, by the alliance which they MAY contract with man, can be made participators of man's immortality. Thus a Nymph or a Sylphide becomes immortal, and capable of the bliss to which we aspire, when she is happy enough to marry one of the "wise;" and a Gnome or a Sylph ceases to be mortal from the moment that he marries one of the daughters of "men."

THE DIVINE MYSTERY. 15

And thus is the mystery solved, in words so plain that any student may understand.

It is here given in a few words and very plainly. This mystery was, to a certain extent, solved by the early church Fathers, as is proven by the work: "Demoniality, or Incubi and Succubi," by the Rev. Father Sinistrari of Ameno. (17th century.)

However, the church Fathers believe that these Elementals, called demons by them, were all wicked; they believed and taught that women bare children from these demons, but that such were always men who were against the Catholic Church, then known as the only TRUE church.

This will be enlarged upon throughout the book, which is really a translation of the work by the Rev. Father Sinistrari, and which is now in such form as is agreeable to our present century. In other words, instead of being called Demons we call them Elementals. The same with other teachings in the book. The body is the same, but it is given in the terms used at the present day.

Beloved Student, you have been given the mystery. You need not believe without knowing like the millions before you. You can KNOW, for herein will you find full instructions so that you may be able to save many of the "Daughters of God."

R. SWINBURNE CLYMER.

 # DEMONIALITY
OR
INCUBI AND SUCCUBI.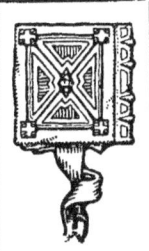

PRELUDE.

ALL theologians have devoted more or less pages to the question of material intercourse between man and the demon. Thick volumes have been written about witchcraft, and the merits of this work were but slender if it merely developed the ordinary thesis; but such is not its characteristic. The ground-matter, from which it derives a truly original and philosophical stamp, is an entirely novel demonstration of the existence of Incubi and Succubi †, as rational animals ‡, both corporal and spiritual like ourselves, living in our midst, being born and dying like us, and lastly redeemed as we are, through the merits of Jesus Christ, and capable of

---

† The reader must bear in mind that these words are no longer used, but that all TRUE Philosophers now call these beings the Elementals. The student must, however, bear in mind the great Rosicrucian Law, i. e., that there are two kinds. The true Elementals known as the Gnomes, Salamanders, Undines and Sylphs, and those disembodied humans who are held to earth through their own misdeeds, passions, crimes, etc., while on earth, who suck out the vitality of negative human beings. These are known as Vampires.

‡ The word "animal" here means human beings. This is proven by the fact that the author says: "Both corporal and spiritual LIKE ourselves."

THE DIVINE MYSTERY.

receiving salvation and damnation †. In the opinion of the Father of Ameno, those beings endowed with sense and reason, thoroughly distinct from angels and demons, pure spirits, are none other than the Fauns, Sylvans and Satyrs of paganism; continued by our Sylphs, Elfs and Goblins; and thus is connected anew THE LINK OF BELIEF. On this score alone, not to mention the interest of details, this book has a charm for the attention of the earnest student.

---

† As explained in the Introduction to this work, and as is still more fully explained in the book "Irreconcilable Gnomes," these beings can become immortal only through the intercession of a human being already immortal.

Man can be saved through the Christ. That is, FINDING THE Christ WITHIN HIMSELF. These Elementals, being of only one of the elements, can naturally not harmonize the other elements, and, therefore, the only way to immortality for them is through the human being who is already immortal. Thus is man saved through the Christ and the Elemental through Man. It is one vast connecting link between the lowest creature and God.

The Divine Mystery.

1. The first author to invent the word Demoniality was no doubt John Caramuel, in his "Fundamental Theology." Before him there is no one who is known to have distinguished that crime from Beastality. All theological moralists, following in the train of St. Thomas, include, under the specific beastiality, "every kind of carnal intercourse with anything whatever of a different species." Such are the words used by St. Thomas. Cajetanus, for instance, in his commentary on that question, classes intercourse with the Demon under the description of beastiality; so does Sylvester, "*De Luxuria*," Bocancia, "*De Matrimonio*."

2. However, it is clear that in the above passage St. Thomas did not at all allude to intercourse with the Demon. As shall be demonstrated further on, that intercourse cannot be included in the very particular species of beastiality; and in order to make that sentence of the holy doctor tally with truth, it must be admitted that when saying of the natural sin, "that committed through the intercourse with a thing of different species, takes the name of beastiality." St. Thomas, by a thing of different species, means a living animal of another species than man; for he could not here use the word *this* in the most general sense, to mean indiscriminately an animate or inanimate being. In fact, if a man should fornicate *cum cadavere human*

THE DIVINE MYSTERY. 23

he would have to do with a thing of a species quite different from his own; similarly *si cadaveri beastiali copularetur;* and yet, *talis coitus* would not be beastiality, but pollution. What, therefore, St. Thomas intended here to specify with preciseness is carnal intercourse with a living thing of a species different from that of man, that is to say, with a beast, and he never in the least thought of intercourse with the Demon.

The subject of beastiality is not a pleasant one, and, since it has no bearing upon the subject in hand at the present time, we will not consider it further. However, it had to be considered this much in order to draw the distinction.

3. Intercourse with the Demon, whether Incubi or Succubi, (which is, properly speaking, as understood by the holy Fathers, Demoniality,) differs in kind from beastiality, and does not in connection with it form one very particular species, as Cajetanus wrongly gives it; for, whatever may have been said to the contrary, some ancients, and later Caramuel in his "Fundamental Theology," unnatural sins differ from each other most distinctly.

Fornication and Sodomy, in most instances, come directly under the head of beastiality. He who is guilty of Sodomy, Onanism and Human Vanpirism cannot become immortal. In fact, these sins will prevent immortality in the human being. On the other hand, Demoniality will bring about immortality to the Elemental. This is to be understood as marriage with the Elemental. Demoniality, as such, has no existence to-day. In fact, it never had, for intercourse with the Elementals is not Demoniality.

4. In sins against nature, the natural semination (which can not be regularly followed by generation) is a genus; but the object of such semination is the difference which marks the species under the genus. Thus, whether semination takes place on the ground, or on an inanimate body, it is pollution, and can lead only to degeneration and eternal death.

5. It is a trite doctrine with Moralists, established by the Council of Trent, session 14, and admitted by theologians that

THE DIVINE MYSTERY.

in confession it suffices to state the circumstances which alter the species of sin. If, therefore, Demoniality and Beastiality belonged to the same very particular species, it would be enough that, each time he has had intercourse with the Demon, the penitent should say to his confessor, "I have been guilty of the sin of beastiality." But this is not so; therefore, those two sins do not belong to the same very particular species.

Churchmen and scientists may deny that man can come into personal intercourse with the Elementals, and to prove this point it is only necessary to quote:

6. St. Austin, who, speaking of carnal intercourse between men and the demon, expresses himself as follows, book 15, chapter 23rd of "The City of God:" "It is widely credited, and such belief is confirmed by the direct or indirect testiony of thoroughly trustworthy people, that Sylvans and Fauns, commonly called Incubi, have frequently molested women, sought and obtained from them coition. There are even Demons, whom the Gauls called Duces or Elfs, who very regulary indulge in those unclean practices; the fact is testified by so many and such weighty authorities that it were imprudent to doubt it."

The student will note that it is plainly stated that the Demon was none other than the Sylvans and Fauns, known later as Duces and Elfs. These are none other than the Elementals. However, the statement made throughout these letters of carnal intercourse, must not be taken too literally, for, though it is true that the Elementals seek *true* marriage with the human family in order to obtain the boon of immortality, it is not true that they seek the human for the mere satisfaction of what would be, to the human, bodily pleasure. The fact is the contrary to this.

THE GREAT LAW.

The Student must bear in mind continually that the holy Fathers, and even early Philosophers, mixed up the Demons (Elementas) with the Vampires (earthbound disembodied Spirits or Souls.)

THE DIVINE MYSTERY.

It is true that those spirits which have left the body of clay, but which are earth-bound on account of crimes, passions, etc., do seek carnal intercourse with the embodied men and women, but this is only for the sake of vampirism. In other words, in order to sap the vitality from humans in order that they may be held near the earth. Such disembodied souls may well be classed as Demons, for they are demons or devils in the true sense. The fact is, the word "fiends" would do greater justice to them. The holy Fathers confounded these Vampires with the Elementals. The Elemental does *not* seek intercourse with humanity in order to satisfy lust or passion, but only so that he or she may become immortal. I hope this matter is plain to the student, and shall now proceed with the work in hand.

7. If the authors be asked how it came to pass that the Demon, who has no body, can have carnal intercourse with man or woman, they unanimously answer that the Demon assumes the corpse of another human being, male or female, as the case may be, or that, from the mixture of materials, he shapes for himself a body endowed with motion, and by means of this he is united with the human being.

Here we have the mystery solved. But here again the authors confound the Elementals with Vampires. No. 7 refers exclusively to such earth-bound souls as before referred to, for the Elemental never takes on a body, and cannot become visible to the human unless that human makes for them the proper surroundings, and even then it is a hard matter. These demons referred to are not Elementals, but disembodied souls who are earth-bound through passions, crimes, etc.

8. We read likewise of numerous women incited to intercourse by the Incubus Demon, and who, though reluctant at first to yield to him, are soon moved by his entreaties, tears and endearments; he is a desperate lover and must not be denied. And although this comes sometimes of the craft of some Wizard who avails himself of the agency of the Demon, yet the Demon not

infrequently acts on his own account.

This again is not an Elemental or Demon, but a disembodied Soul or Vampire. The Elemental never work in this manner, and never seek the human in this way.

9. Now, it is undoubted by theologians and philosophers that intercourse between mankind and the Demon sometimes gives birth to human beings; that is how is to be born the Antichrist, according to some doctors, such as Bellarmin, Suarez, Maluenda, etc. They further observe that, from a natural cause, the children thus begotten by Incubi are tall, very hardy, very proud and wicked. Thus writes Maluenda; as for the cause, he gives it from Vallesius, Archphysician in Reggio.

This now *does* refer to the Elementals, for there can be no issue from the intercourse between the human and disembodied Soul or Vampire. The Fathers admit that these children may be powerful, but as this is not in accord with their belief, they naturally claim that such children will be very wicked. This is really not true. In fact, absolutely the contrary is true. Why? Because the Elementals have no gross material in their beings, therefore absolutely no lust. They are simply one pure element. Consequently the issue between them and a human must be very rare, very pure, since all the carnal desires that such a child can have must come altogether from the mother. Consequently, only Christs or Saviours can be born through such intercourse, and, as the male Elementals are very few, such births happen but seldom. Let us see the list as given by the holy Father:

10. Maluenda shows from the testimony of various authors, mostly classical, that such associations gave birth to: Romulus Remus, according to Livy and Plutarch; Servius-Tullius, the sixth king of Rome, according to Dyonisius of Halicarnassus and Pliny the Elder; Plato the Philosopher, according to Diogenes Laertius and Saint Hieronymus; Alexander the Great, according to Plutarch and Quintus-Curtius; Seleucus, king of Syria, according to Justinus and Appianus; Scipio Africanus the Elder, according to Livy; the Emperor Cæsar Augustus, according to Suetonius; Aristomenes the Messenian, an illustrious

THE DIVINE MYSTERY. 31

Greek commander, according to Strabo and Pausanias; as also Merlin or Melchin, the Englishman, born from an Incubus and a nun, the daughter of Charlemagne; and, lastly, as shown by the writings of Cochloeus, quoted by Maluenda, that damned Heresiarchycleped Martin Luther.

Certainly a strong list, but, none the less, one that can be mainly true; and now, my Christian friends, if Martin Luther was the offspring of a Virgin and an Elemental, *why not the Christ?* The student must bear in mind the one Great Law: namely, that the human mind cannot imagine anything which has no foundation in fact. The Great Law of Hermes is: "As above so below; as below so above." "As in the Material so in the Spiritual." Therefore, that which the mind of man can conceive, can also be brought into material manifestation.

I do not say that Martin Luther was thus born, but I say this, and I challenge the Christian world, Catholic or Protestant, to successfully contradict me, that Christ was *thus* born. If he were not, then the Doctrine of the Immaculate Conception is a lie, and if this is a lie, then the very foundation of religion, both Protestant and Catholic, is a lie and a farce.

11. Although it is generally admitted as a fact that those who are thus begotten excel other men, yet such superiority is not always shown by their vices, but sometimes by their virtues and even their morals. Scipio Africanus, for instance, Cæsar Augustus and Plato the Philosopher, as is recorded of each of them respectively by Livy, Suetonius and Diogenes Laertius, had excellent morals. Whence may be inferred that, if other individuals begotten in the same way have been downright villians, it was not owing to their being born of an Incubi, but to their having, of their own free will, chosen to be such.

Surely this is a confession for a Church Father to make, and this proves just exactly what I have already proven. If these great men were born, then it is an easy matter for a Christ or a Buddha to have been thus born.

12. We also read in the Testament, Genesis, 6, verse 4, that

giants were born when the sons of God came in unto the daughters of men; that is the very letter of the sacred text. Now, these giants were men of *great stature*, says Baruch, Chapter 3, verse 26, and far superior to other men. Not only were they distinguished by their hugh size, but also by their physical power. Some contend that by sons of God are meant the sons of Seth, and by daughters of men the daughters of Cain, because the former practiced piety, religion and every other virtue, whilst the descendents of Cain were quite the reverse; but, with all due reverence to Chrysostom, Cyrillus, Hilarius, and others, who were of that opinion, it must be conceded that it clashes with the obvious meaning of the text. Scripture says, in fact, that of the conjunction of the above mentioned were born men of hugh bodily size; consequently, those giants were not previously in existence, and if their birth was the result of that conjunction, it cannot be ascribed to the intercourse of the sons of Seth with the daughters of Cain, who being of ordinary stature, could but procreate children of ordinary stature. Therefore, if the intercourse in question gave birth to beings of hugh stature, the reason is that it was not the common connection between man and woman, but the performance of the Incubi Demons, who, from their nature, may very well be styled Sons of God. Such is the opinion of the Platonist Philosophers and of Francis Georges, the Venetian; nor is it discrepant with that of Josephus the Historian, Philo the Jew, St. Justinus the Martyr, Clement of Alexandria, and Tertullian, who look upon Incubi as corporal Angels who have allowed themselves to fall i ito the sin of lewdness with women. Indeed, as shall be shown hereafter, though seemingly distinct, these two opinions are but one and the same.

This really refer to the Elementals. It is not true that these Elementals allowed themselves to fall into lewdness. It is that they desired to become Immortal that they undertook these intercourses, and there is not a single instance in history to prove fhat an Elemental had intercourse more than once with a woman. Were lewdness the object then this would not be true,

THE DIVINE MYSTERY. 35

13. If these incubi, in conformity with the general belief, have begotten Giants by means of the Vita taken from man, it is impossible, as aforesaid, that of that Vita should have been born any but men of approximately the same size as he from whom it came; for it would be in vain for the Demon, when acting the part of a Succubus, to draw from man an unwonted qualific of the Vita liquor in order to procreate therefrom children of higher stature. Quality has nothing to do here, since all depends, as has been said, upon the vitality of the Vita, not its quality. We are, therefore, bound to infer that Giants are born of another sperm than man's, and that, consequently, the Incubus, for the purpose of generation, uses Vita which is not man's.

14. Subject to correction from our Holy Mother Church, and as a mere expression of opinion, I say that the Incubus when having intercourse, begets the human fetus from his own Vita.

In this the Father is correct. However, it is a fact that the Vampires obtain their vitality through the human for this reason, they use Sodomites, Onanits, and others of this ilk. It is also for this reason that the human who practices these things gradually throws away his Soul and feeds these Vampires. Such a human gradually destroys all chances of Immortality, and this is the sin that God will not forgive. It is not that He could not forgive it, but it is because such threw their very Soul away until there is nothing left but the mere body, the shell. The Soul has been absorbed by Vampires.

15. I premise, as an article of belief, that there are purely spiritual creatures, not in any way partaking of corporal matter as was ruled by the Council of Lateran, under the pontificate of Innocent III. Such are the blessed Angels, and the Demons condemned to everlasting fire. Some Doctors, it is true, have professed, subsequently even to this Council, that the spirituality of Angels and Demons is not an article of belief. Others even have asserted that they are corporal, whence Bonaventure Baron has drawn the conclusion that it is neither heretical nor erroneous to ascribe to Angels or Demons a twofold substance, corporal and spiritual. Yet the Council having formally de-

THE DIVINE MYSTERY. 37

clared it to be an article of belief that God *is the maker of all things visible and invisible, spiritual and corporal, who has raised from nothing every creature spiritual or corporal, Angelic or Terrestrial*, I contend it is an article of belief that there are certain merely spiritual creatures, and that such are Angels; not all of them, but a certain number.

The student must bear in mind that here are really meant the Angels, on the one hand, which are good and evil forces; Devils, on the other hand, which are bad. The word Demon does not here signify the same thing that it did when used before. Here it means the evil side.

16. It may seem strange, yet it must be admitted not to be unlikely. If, in fact, theologians concur in establishing among Angels a specific, and therefore essential, diversity so considerable that, according to St. Thomas, there are not two Angels of the same species, but that each of them is a species by himself, why not certain Angels be more pure spirit, of a consequently very superior nature, and others corporal, therefore of a less perfect nature, differing thus from each other in their corporal or incorporal substance? This doctrine has the advantage of solving the otherwise insoluble contradiction between two OEcumenical Councils, namely, the Seventh General Synod and the above-mentioned Council of Lateran. For, during the fifth sitting of the Synod, the second of Nicea, a book was introdued written by John of Thessalonica against a pagan philosopher, wherein occur the following propositions: "Respecting Angels, Archangels and their powers, to which I adjoin our own Souls, the Catholic Church is really of opinion that they are intelligences, but not entirely bodiless and senseless, as you Gentiles aver. She, on the contrary, ascribes to them a subtile body, aerial or igneous, according to what is written: He makes the spirits His Angels, and the burning fire His Minister." And, further on, "Although not corporal in the same way as ourselves, made of the *four* elements, yet it is impossible to say that Angels, Demons and Souls are incorporal, for they have been seen many a time, invested with their own bodies, by those whose eyes the Lord has opened." And after that book had

THE DIVINE MYSTERY.

been read through before all the Fathers in Council assembled, Tharasius, the Patriarch of Constantinople, submitted it to the approval of the Council, with these words: "The Father showeth that Angels should be pictured, since their form can be defined, and they have been seen in the shape of men." Without a dissent the Synod answered: "Yes, my Lord."

This explains itself, except that it is remarkable in that the composition of both man and the Elementals was understood. "Made in the same way as ourselves, *made of the four elements.*" It is in this that man differs from the Elemental. Man is made of the four elements, and, consequently, is both mortal and Immortal. The Fire, or element of Fire, gives him his soul, his power to love and his Immortality. The Elementals are only of one element, and, consequently, unless they can come into natural connection with a human being cannot be Immortal.

They have been seen by "those whose eyes the Lord had opened." This also is true. When man, through certain Soul development, has reached a state where the Spiritual Sight is opened, he can see, not only the Angels, which are distinct from the Elementals, but he can see the Elementals also. This is no idle dream, as the writer knows many who can and do hold daily intercourse with these Elementals, and knows of one Initiate who has been instrumental in bringing about the Immortality of more than one hundred Elementals of Fire.

The Angels must not be confounded with the Elementals, for all Angels are eternal in that they are the messengers of God. Such Angels may and do appear to men, but they have no intercourse with men, since there is no need of it, and, therefore, no desire. Desire is the *law that rules* in all things.

17. I premise that the word Angel applies not indeed to the kind, but to the office. The Holy Fathers are agreed thereupon. (St. Ambrose, on the "Epistle to the Hebrews;" St. Austin, "City of God;" St. Gregory, "Homily 34 on Scripture," St. Isidorus, "Supreme Goodness.") An Angel, very truly says St. Ambrose, is thus styled, not because he is a spirit, but on account of his office. Nuntius in Latin, that is to say, *Messen-*

THE DIVINE MYSTERY. 41

ger. It follows that whoever is entrusted by God with a mission, be he spirit or man, may be called an Angel, and is thus called in the Holy Scriptures, where the following words are applied to Priests, Preachers and Doctors, who, as Messengers of God, explain to men the Divine Will. (Malachi, chapter 2; v. 7.) "The Priest's lips should keep knowledge, and they should seek the law at his mouth, for he is the Angel of the Lord of Hosts." The same prophet, chapter 3; v. 1, bestows the name of Angel on St. John the Baptist, when saying: "Behold, I will send my Angel, and he shall prepare the way before me." That this prophecy literally applies to St. John the Baptist is testified by our Lord Jesus Christ in the Gosple according to St. Matthew, chapter 11; v. 10. Still more: "God himself is called an Angel, because he has been sent by His Father to herald the law of mercy. To witness, the prophecy of Isiah, chapter 9; v. 6, according to the Septuagint, "He shall be called an Angel of Wonderful Counsel." And more plainly still in Malachi, chapter 3; v. 1: "The Lord whom you seek shall suddenly come to his temple, even the Angel of the covenant whom ye delight in," a prophecy which literally applies to our Lord Jesus Christ. There is, consequently, nothing absurd in the contention that some Angels are corporal, since men, who assuredly have a body, are called Angels.

18. I premise that Holy Scripture and ecclesiastical tradition do not teach us anything beyond what is required for the salvation of the soul, namely, Faith, Hope and Charity. Consequently. from a thing not long being stated, either by Scripture or tradition, it must not be inferred that that thing is not in existence. For instance, Faith teaches us that God, by His Word made things visible and invisible, and also that through the merits of our Lord Jesus Christ, grace and glory are conferred on every rational creature. Now, that there is another world than the one we live in, and that it be peopled by men not born of Adam, but made by God in some other way, as is implied by those who believe the lunar globe to be inhabited; or, further, that in the very world we dwell in, there be other rational creatures besides man and the Angelic Spirits, creatures general-

ly invisible to us, and whose being is disclosed but accidently, through the instrumentality of their own power. All that has nothing to do with Faith, and the knowledge or ignorance thereof is no more necessary to the salvation of man than knowing the number or nature of all physical things.

19. I premise that neither philosophy nor theology is repugnant to the possible existence of rational creatures having spirit and body and distinct from man. Such repugnance could be supported only on God, and that is inadmisable, since He is all-mighty, or on the thing to be made, and that likewise can not be supported, for, as there are purely spiritual creatures, such as Angels, or merely material, such as the world, or lastly, semi-spiritual and semi-corporal, or an earthly and gross corporeity, such as man, so there may *well be in existence a creature endowed with a rational spirit and a corporeity less gross and more subtile than man's.*

20. Question: Should such creatures be styled rational animals? And, if so, in what do they differ from man, with whom they would have that definition in common?

21. Yes, they would be rational animals, provided with senses and organs even as man. They would, however, differ from man not only in the more subtile nature, but also in the matter of their bodies. In fact, as shown by Scripture, man has been made from the grossest of all elements, namely clay, a gross mixture of water and earth. But those creatures would be made from the *most subtile part of all elements,* or of one or other of them.

Thus some would proceed from earth, others from water, or air, or fire; and in order that they should not be defined in the same terms as man, to the definition of the latter should be added the mention of the gross materiality of his body, wherein he would differ from said animals.

22. Question: At what period would those animals have been originated, and where from? From earth, like the beasts, or from water, like quadrupeds, birds, etc.? Or, on the contrary, would they have been made, like man, by our Lord God?

THE DIVINE MYSTERY. 45

23. Answer: It is an article of belief, expressly laid down by the Council of Lateran, that whatever is in fact and at present, was made in the origin of the world. By His all-mighty virtue, God, from the beginning of time, raised together from nothing both orders of creatures, spiritual and corporal. Now, those animals also would be included in the generality of creatures. As to their formation, it might be said that God Himself, through the medium of Angels, made their body as He did man's, to which *an Immortal spirit was to be united*. That body being of a nobler nature than that of other animals, it was meet that it should be united to an incorporal and highly noble spirit.

24. Question: Would those animals descend from one individual, as all men descended from Adam; or, on the contrary, would many have been made at the same time, as was the case for the other living things issued from earth and water, wherein were males and females for the preservation of the kind by generation? Would there be amongst them a distinction between the sexes? Would they be subject to birth and death, to senses, passions, want of food, power of growth? If so, what their nutrition? Would they lead a social life, as men do? By what laws ruled? Would they build up cities for their dwellings, cultivate the arts and sciences, hold property, and wage war between themselves, as men are wont to do?

25. It may be that all descend from one individual, as man descended from Adam. It may be, also, that a number of males and females were made initially, who preserved their kind by generation. We will further admit that they were born and die; that they are divided into males and females, and are moved by senses and passions, as men are; that they feed and grow according to the size of their body. Their food, however, instead of being gross, like that required by the human body, must be delicate and vapory, emanating through spirituous effluvia from whatever in the physical world abounds with highly volatile corpuscles, such as the flavor of meats, the fume of wine, the fragrancy of fruit, flowers, aromatics, which evolve an abundance of those effluvia until all their subtile and volatile parts

have completely evaporated. To their being able to lead a social life, with distinctions of rank and precedence; to their cultivating the arts and sciences, exercising functions, maintaining armies, building up cities, doing, in short, whatever is requisite for their preservation, I have in the main no objection.

I would refer the student to the book "The Irreconcilable Gnome" for the reason *why* there are Elementals, or why the Elementals are not human in every sense as we are. I would, also, refer the student to the private work "The Mysteries of Osiris" for the explanation of the first "fall" of man.

What the Father has to say regarding the food of the Elementals, is entirely and absolutely correct. This explains why, in the process of Soul Development, the Neophyte uses incense. Using incense has a triple meaning. It helps the Neophyte to open the Soul sight; it attracts the Elementals because it proves to them that there is one who desires their companionship, and it is also a food for them.

The Father here further clears the question as to the difference between the Elementals and the Vampires, or disembodied souls.

The Elementals do not live upon the vitality of humanity, but upon such food as before stated. The Vampires live entirely upon human vitality.

A MYSTERY.

It is a well known fact that seldom is a drunkard killed while in a drunken state. It does not matter into how dangerous a place he may go, he usually comes out safe. This is the reason: When a man is drunk he is in an entirely negative state. While in this state, more especially if stupefied, these disembodied souls, who are earth-bound, can easily absorb the vitality they require in order to live. This they do, and it is, therefore, to their great benefit to see that such a slave is not killed, for were he or she killed their food would at once cease, and it would mean their death. It is, therefore, their desire that such negatives—Vampire slaves—shall not come to any harm,

and they watch over them carefully.

Sooner or later, they have accomplished their desire and no longer need such a negative. The result is that they no longer protect such drunkard, and death comes while he is in some drunken state, and the verdict is "heart failure."

This is also the reason why it is so hard to reform a drunkard. He may stop for months at a time, but it is only by exerting his will that he can keep away from drink. There is always that "something" urging him to drink, until this desire becomes so powerful that he will start drinking again.

The greater part of Mediumship also comes under the same heading. The vast majority of mediums are not honest, neither are they living a pure life. These disembodied Vampires come into touch with them because they are Negatives. They give them a certain amount of knowledge, in exchange for which they receive enough vitality to live. Gradually the medium becomes so absolutely sucked dry of vitality that there is a physical and mental breakdown.

I naturally do not refer to that pure, conscious mediumship where the medium is both pure, developed and honest, but to that universal, commercial mediumship abounding on every hand.

26. Question: What would their figure be—human or otherwise?

27. As regards their figure, we neither can or should be affirmative, since it escapes our senses, being too delicate for our sight or touch. That we must leave to themselves, and to such as have the privilege of *intuitive* acquaintance with immaterial substance. But, so far as probability goes, I say that their figure tallies with the human body, save some distinctive peculiarity, should the very tenuity of their bodies not be deemed sufficient. I am led to that consideration that of all the works of God, the human frame is the most perfect, and that whilst all other animals stoop to the ground, because their soul is mortal,

THE DIVINE MYSTERY. 51

God, as Ovid, the poet, says, in his "Metamorphoses,"
"Gave man an erect figure, bidding him behold
    the heavens,
And raise his face towards the stars,"
man's soul having been made Immortal for the heavenly bode. Considering that the animals we are speaking of would be gifted with a spirit immaterial, rational and Immortal, capable, therefore, of beatitude and damnation, it is proper to admit that the body to which that spirit is united may be like unto the most *noble* animal (man) frame, that is to say, to the human frame. Whence it follows that in the diverse parts of that body there must be an essential order; that the foot, for instance, can not be an appendage to the head, nor the hand to the belly, but that each organ is in its right place, according to the functions it has to perform. As to the constitutive parts of these organs, it is, in my opinion, necessary that there should be some more or less strong, others more or less slender, in order to meet the requirements of the organic working. Nor can this be fairly objected to on the ground of the slenderness of the bodies themselves; for the strength or thickness of the organic parts alluded to would not be absolute, but merely in comparison with the more slender ones. That, moreover, may be observed in all natural fluids, such as wine, oil, milk, etc., however homogeneous and similar to each other their component parts may look, yet they are not so, for some are clayish, others aqueous. There are fixed salts, volatile salts, all of which are made obvious by a chemical analysis. So it would be in our case, for, supposing the bodies of those animals to be as subtile and slender as the natural fluids, air, water, etc., there would nevertheless be discrepancies in the quality of their constitutive parts, some of which would be strong when compared with others more slender, although the whole body which they compose might be called slender.

The Elementals are formed like the human form, except that their bodies are far more perfect. They are composed of only the pure elements, no gross material entering their make-up, consequently they can be as perfect as they wish. On the oth-

er hand, there being no material or gross matter in their make-up, they may appear in different forms in different people.

It is with pleasure that we here give the picture of one of the Elementals of Fire, the Salamanderine. This is from that beautiful work, "The Salamanderine," which we hope to issue at an early date.

The student should carefully note the statement: "That we must leave to themselves, and to such as have the privilege of *intuitive* acquaintance with immaterial substances." This, from a holy Father, is of vast importance. It is really through the Intuitive faculty that one can first become acquainted with the Elementals. This can come only through Soul development.

28. Question: Would these animals be subject to diseases, infirmities, sleep, food, drink, etc.?

THE DIVINE MYSTERY. 55

29. Their bodies, though subtile, being material, they would, of course, be liable to decay. They might, therefore, suffer from adverse agencies, and consequently, be diseased; that is, their organs might not perform, or painfully and imperfectly perform the office assigned to them, for therein consist all diseases whatever with certain animals, as has been distinctly explained by the illustrious Michael Ettmullat, "Physiology," C. V. thesis I. In sooth, their bodies being less gross than the human frame, comprising less elements mixed together, they would not so easily suffer from adverse influences, and would, therefore, be less liable to disease than man. Their life would also exceed his, for the more perfect an animal, as a species, the longer i s days. Thus mankind whose existence extends beyond that of other animals. For I do not believe in the centenary existence of crows, stags, ravens, and the like, of which Pliny tells his customary stories; and although his dreams have been re-echoed by others without previous inquiry, it is no less clear that before writing thus, not one has faithfully noted the birth or death of those animals. They have been content with taking up the strange fable, as has been the case with the Phenix, whose longevity is discarded as a story by Tacitus, "Annals," B. 6. It were, therefore, to be inferred that the animals we are speaking of would live longer still than man, for, as shall be said hereafter, they would be more *noble* than he. Consequently, also, would be subject to the other bodily affections, and require rest and food. Now, as rational beings, amenable to discipline, they might also continue ignorant, if their minds did not receive the culture of study and instruction, and some amongst them would be more or less versed in science, more or less clever, according as their intelligence had been more or less trained. However, generally speaking, and considering the whole of the species, they would be more learned than men, not from the subtility of their bodies, but perhaps because of the greater activity of their minds or the longer space of their life, which would enable them to learn more things than men. Such are, indeed, the motives assigned by St. Austin ("Divin. Demon." Ch. 3, and "Spirit and Soul," Ch. 37), to the prescience of the future in

THE DIVINE MYSTERY.

Demons. They might indeed suffer from natural agencies, but they could hardly be killed, on account of the speed with which they can escape from danger.

In the main, the holy Father is right in his conclusions. However, these Elementals do not suffer from diseases, for the reason that a single Element cannot suffer. Before man fell into the material form, he felt neither sorrow or joy. Consequently he *desired* to know. Through this desire he fell into the material form with all its sorrows and joys. The Elemental does not suffer from disease. Its death is a natural death from old age, as should be the death of man. However, immediately that an Elemental has been married with the human, it will know both sorrow and joy, and be subject to nearly all the sorrows and pains of the human. This is the Law.

30. Would these animals be born in original sin, and have been redeemed by the Lord Christ? Would the grace have been conferred upon them, and through what sacrament? Under what law would they live, and would they be capable of beatitude and damnation?

31. It is an article of belief that Christ has merited grace and glory for all rational creatures without exception. It is also an article of belief that glory is not conferred on a rational creature until such creature has been previously endowed with grace, which is the disposition of glory. According to a like article, glory is conferred by merits. Now, these merits are grounded on the perfect observance of the commands of God, which is accomplished through grace. The above questions are thus solved. Whether those creatures did or did not sin originally is uncertain. It is clear, however, that if their first parent had sinned as Adam sinned, his descent would be born in original sin, as men are born. And, as God never leaves a rational creature without a remedy, so long as it treads the way, if these creatures were infected with original or actual sin, God would have provided them with a remedy; but whether it is the case, and of what kind is the remedy, is a secret between God and them. Surely, if they had sacraments identical with or different from those in use in the human Church militant, for the

THE DIVINE MYSTERY.

institution and efficacy thereof they would be indebted to the merits of Jesus Christ, the Redeemer and Universal Atoner of rational creatures. It would likewise be highly proper, nay necessary, that they should live under some law given them by God, and through the observance of which they might merit beatitude. But what would be that law, whether merely natural or written, Mosaic or Evangelical, or different from all these and specially instituted by God, that we are ignorant of.

The author came near to the solution of the problem, and especially concerning the original sin.

The Elementals were *not* born in original sin, for if they had been then they would be mortal like man. This in itself is the strong proof that they were *not* born in original sin. Why they are Elementals instead of men is clearly given in "The Irreconcilable Gnome."

They cannot be redeemed through Christ, but must be redeemed through the agency of man. Man must be their redeemer. This has already been fully explained. The Laws of God as given to man cannot affect them, nor the sacraments. Man alone, as already explained, must be their Savior. There is no damnation for them. They must either become Immortal through man or they die.

32. The only argument, and that a rather lame one, which long meditations have suggested to me against the possibility of such creatures, is that, if they really existed in the world, we should find them mentioned somewhere by Philosophers, Holy Scriptures, Ecclesiastical Tradition, or the Holy Fathers. Such not being the case, their utter impossibility should be inferred.

33. But that argument which, in fact, calls in question their existence rather than their possibility, is easily disposed of by our premises, for no argument can stand in virtue of a negative authority. Besides, it is not correct to assert that neither the Philosophers, nor the Scriptures, nor the Fathers have handed down any notion of them. Plato, as is reported by Apuleius, "The Demon of Socrates;" and Plutarch, "Isis and Osiris," de-

clared that Demons were beings of animal kind, passive souls, rational intelligences, aerial bodies, everlasting; and they gave them the name of Demons, which of itself is nowise offensive, since it means
REPLETE WITH WISDOM.
So that when authors allude to the Devil (or Evil Angel) they do not merely call him Demon, but Cacodemon; and say likewise Eudemon, when speaking of a good Angel. Those creatures are also mentioned in Scripture and by the Fathers.

34. Now, that we have proved that those creatures are possible, let us go a step further, and show that they exist. Taking for granted the truth of the recitals concerning the intercourse of Incubi and Succubi with mortals, recitals so numerous that it would look like impudence to deny the fact, as is stated by St. Austin, whose testimony is given, I argue: Where the peculiar passion of the sense is found, there, also, of necessity, is the sense itself; for, according to the principles of philosophy, the peculiar passion flows from nature, that is to say, where the acts and operations of the sense are found, there also is the sense, operations and acts being but its external form. Now, those Incubi and Succubi present acts, operations, peculiar passions, which spring from the senses. They are, therefore, endowed with senses. But senses cannot exist without concomitant composite organs, without a combinations of soul and body. Incubi and Succubi have, therefore, soul and body, and, consequently, are animals: but their acts and operations are, also, those of a rational soul. Their soul is, therefore, rational, and thus, from first to last, they are rational animals.

The student must read "Spirits" for "Soul," for if these Elementals had a soul they would be Immortal. They have body and spirit, but the soul, the immortal part, can only come through marriage with the human, or that which already is Immortal.

35. The Evil Spirits, the incorporal Demons, which have to do with Black Magicians and Sorcerism, constrain them to demon worship, to the abjuration of the Orthodox Faith, to the commission of enchantments and foul crimes, as preliminary

conditions to the infamous intercourse. Now, Incubi pretend to *nothing of the kind*. These are, therefore, *no evil spirits*. Lastly, as written by Guaccius, at the mere utterance of the name of Jesus or Mary, at the sign of the Cross, the approach of holy relics or consecrated objects, at exorcisms, at adjurations or priestly injunctions, the Evil Demon either shudders or takes to flight, or is agitated and howls, as is daily seen with energumens and is shown by numerous narratives of Gauccius cencerning the nightly revels of Black Magicians and unholy Mediums. The Incubi, on the contrary, stand all those ordeals without taking to flight or showing the least fear.

36. Now, if the evil Demons, subdued by our Lord Jesus Christ, are stricken by fear by his name, the cross and the holy things; if, on the other hand, the good Angels rejoice at these same things without, however, inciting men to sin nor to give offense to God, whilst the Incubi, without having any dread of the holy things, provoke to intercourse, it is clear that they are *neither evil Demons nor good Angels*. But *it is also clear that they are not men, though endowed with reason*. What, then, are they? Supposing them to have reached the goal, and to be pure spirits, they would be damned or blessed, for correct theology does not admit of pure spirits on the way to salvation. If damned, they would revere the name and the cross of Christ; if blessed, they would not incite men to intercourse. They would, therefore, be different from pure spirits, and thus have a body, and be on the way to salvation.

37. As an other principal proof of our conclusion regarding the existence of these animals, in other words, respecting the corporeity of Incubi, is adduced by the testimony of St. Hieronymus in his "Life of St. Paul, the First Hermit." St. Anthony, says he, set out on a journey to visit St. Paul. After traveling several days he met a Centaur, of whom he inquired the hermet's abode. Whereupon the Centaur, growling some uncouth and scarcely intelligible answer, shew the way with his outstretched hand, and fled with the utmost speed into a wood. The Holy Abbott kept on his way, and, in a dale, met a litt'e man, almost a dwarf, with creeked hands, horned brow, and

his lower extremities ending with goats' feet. At the sight of him, St. Anthony stood still, and, fearing the arts of the Devil, comforted himself with a sign of the cross. But, far from running away, or even seeming frightened at it, the little fellow respectfully approached the old man, and tendered him as a peace offering dates for his journey. The blessed St. Anthony then inquired who he was. "I am a mortal," replied he, "and one of the inhabitants of the Wilderness, whom Gentility, under its varied delusions, worships under the names of Fauns, Satyrs and Incubi. I am on a mission from my flock. We request thee to pray for us unto the common God, whom ye know to have come for the salvation of the world, and whose praise is sounded all over the earth." Rejoicing at the glory of Christ, St. Anthony, turning his face towards Alexandria, and striking the ground with his staff, cried out: "Woe be unto thee, thou harlot city, who worshipest animals as Gods!" Such is the narrative of St. Hieronymus, who expatiates at length on the fact, explaining its import in a long discourse.

38. It were indeed rash to doubt the truth of the above recital, constantly referred to by the greatest of the Doctors of the Holy Church, of St. Hieronymus, whose authority no Catholic will ever deny. Let us, therefore, investigate the circumstances thereof which must clearly confirm our opinion.

39. We must observe that if ever a saint was assailed by the arts of the Demon, saw throw his infernal devices, and carried off victories and trophies from the contest, that saint was St. Anthony, as is shown by his life, written by St. Athanasius. Now, since in that little man St. Anthony did not recognize a devil but an animal, saying, "Woe unto thee, thou harlot city, who worshipest animals as Gods!" it is clear that it was no devil or pure spirit ejected from heaven and damned, but some kind of an animal. Still more. St. Anthony, when instructing his friars and cautioning them against the assaults of the Demon, said to them, as related in the Roman Breviary "Festival of St. Anthony, Abbot," B. 1.) "Believe me, my brethren, Satan dreads the vigils of pious men, their prayers, fasts, voluntary poverty, compassion and humility; but, above all, he dreads

their burning love of our Lord Christ, at the mere sign of whose most Holy Cross he flies disabled." As the little man, against whom St. Anthony guarded himself with a sign of the cross, neither took fright nor fled, but approached the Saint confidently and humbly, offering him some dates, it is a sure sign that he was no Devil.

40. We must observe that the little man said "I am a mortal," whence it follows that he was an animal subject to death, and, consequently, called into being through generation. For an immeterial spirit is immortal, because simple, and, consequently, is not called into being through generation from preexistent matter, but through creation, and, consequently, also, cannot lose it through the corruption called death. Its existence can only come to an end through annihilation. Therefore, when saying he was mortal, he professed himself an animal.

41. We must observe that he said he knew that the common God had suffered in human flesh. Those words show him to have been a rational animal, for brutes know nothing but what is sensible and present, and can, therefore, have no knowledge of God. If that little man said that he and his fellows were aware of God having suffered in human flesh, it shows that, by means of some revelation, he had acquired the notion of God as we have ourselves the revealed faith. That God assumed human flesh, and suffered in it, is the essence of the two principal articles of our Faith—the existence of God, one and threefold; His Incarnation, Passion, and Resurrection. All that shows, as I said, that it was a rational animal, capable of the knowledge of God through revelation, like ourselves, and endowed with a rational and, consequently, immortal soul.

42. We must observe that, in the name of his whole flock, whose delegate he professed to be, he besought St. Anthony to pray for them to the common God. Whereupon I infer that that little man was capable of beatitude and damnation, and that he was not *in termino*, but *in via*.

Here is the proof of one thing which I have always contended for. If these Elementals could become Immortal through their own efforts, it would not be necessary for them to appeal

THE DIVINE MYSTERY. 69

to the human beings for such prayer. They would then go direct to the Godhead for their salvation, or Regeneration. This is not possible. Consequently there is but one way. They must appeal to mankind, and man must help them to Immortality. It is the only way for them.

43. We must observe that the little man professed to be delegated by others of his kind, when saying, "I am on a mission from my flock," words from which many inferences may be deduced. One is, that the little man was not alone of his kind, an exceptional and solitary monster, but that there were many of the same species, since congregating they made up a flock, and that he came in the name of all; which could not have been, had not the will of the many centered in him. Another is, that those animals held a social life, since one of them was sent in the name of the many. Another is, that, although living in the Wilderness, it is not assigned to them as a permanent abode; for St. Anthony having never previously been in that desert, which was far distant from his hermitage, they could not have known whom he was, nor what his degree of sanctity. It was, therefore, necessary that they should become acquainted with him elsewhere, and, consequently, that they should have travelled beyond that Wilderness.

44. We must observe that the little man said he was one of those whom "the Gentiles, blinded by error, called Fauns, Satyrs and Incubi;" and by these words is shown the truth of our principal proposition, that Incubi are rational animals, capable of beatitude and damnation.

45. The apparation of such little men is of frequent occurrence in metalic mines, as is written by Gregorius Agsicola, in his book "De Animal-Subterran." They appear to the miners clothed like themselves, play and caper together, laugh and titter, and throw stones at them for the sake of amusement. A sign, says the above named author, of excellent success, and of the finding of some branch or body of a mineral tree.

This is true, but only one kind of Elementals can ever be found in the mines. These are the "Gnomes," or Elementals of the earth.

THE DIVINE MYSTERY.

46. The only question which remains to be answered is this: Whence do those little men, or Incubi, dwell? To that I reply: Some are earthly, some aqueous, some aerial, some igneous; that is to say, that their bodies are made of the most subtile parts of the elements. Their dwellings will, consequently, be found in that element which corresponds to their bodies. Igneous Incubi, for instance, will only stay forcibly, may be will not stay at all, in water or marshes, which are adverse to them, Thus with the others also. We see the like happen to men, who, accustomed to thicker air, cannot reach certain lofty ridges of the Alps, where the air is too subtile for their lungs.

47. St. Austin, then, in his "Commentary on Genesis," book 2, chapter 17, writes as follows concerning Demons: "They have the knowledge of some truths, partly through the more subtile acumen of their senses, partly through the greater subtility of their bodies," and book 3, chapter 1, "Demons are aerial animals, because they partake of the nature of aerial bodies." In his Epistle 115 to Hebridius he affirms that they are "aerial or ethereal animals, endowed with very sharp senses." In the "City of God," book 11, chapter 13, he says that "The worst Demon has an aerial body." Book 21, chapter 10, he writes: The bodies of certain Demons, as has been believed by some learned men, are even made of the thick and damp air which we breathe." Book 15, chapter 23: "He dares not define whether Angels, with an aerial body, could feel the lust which would incite them to communicate with women." Psalm 14, he observes that "the body of Angels is inferior to the soul." And in his book "De Divinit Daemonum" he everywhere, and especially chapter 23, teaches that "Demons have subtile bodies."

Regarding the food of the Elementals, or Incubi, let us see to this, also.

48. I deduce that, being animals, consequently reproducible through generation and liable to corruption, they require food for the restoration of their corporal substance wasted by effluvia. For the life of every sensible being consists in nothing else but the motion of the corporal elements which flow and

ebb, are acquired, lost and recruited by means of substances spirituous, yet material, assimilated by the living things, either through inhalation of air or by the fermentation of food which spiritualizes its substance.

49. But their bodies being subtile, equally subtile and delicate must be its food. And, just as perfumes and other vaporous and volatile substances, when adverse to their nature, offend and put them to flight, in the like manner, when agreeable, they delight in and feed upon them. Now, as is written by Cornelius, "Manna is nothing but an emanation of water and earth, refined and baked by the heat of the sun, and then coagulated and condensed by the cold of the following night." Of course, I am speaking of the manna sent down from Heaven for the nourishment of the Hebrews, and which differs, all in all, from nostrate or medicinal manna. The latter, in fact, according to Ettmuller, "is merely the juice or transudation of certain trees which, during the night, gets mixed up with dew, and, the next morning, coagulates and thickens in the heat of the sun." The manna of the Hebrews, on the contrary, derived from other principles, far from coagulating, liquified in the heat of the sun, as is shown in Scripture. The manna of the Hebrews was, therefore, undoubtedly of the most subtile substance, consisting as it did of emanations of earth and water, and being dissolved by the sun and made to disappear. Consequently, it may well have been the food of the animals we are speaking of, and thus have been truly called by David "Bread of Angels."—

50. We have another authority in the Gospel according to St. John, chapter 10, verse 16, where it is said: "And other sheep I have, which are not of this fold. Them I must bring, and they shall hear my voice, and they shall have one fold and one shepherd." If we inquire what are those sheep which are of that fold, and what the fold of which the Lord Christ speaketh, we are answered by all commentators that the only fold of Christ is the Church to which the preaching of the Gospel was to bring the Gentiles, sheep of another fold than that of the Hebrews. They are, in fact, of opinion that the fold of Christ was the Synagogue, because David had said, Psalm 95, verse 7:

THE DIVINE MYSTERY.

"We are the people of his pasture, and the sheep of his hand." And, also, because Abraham and David had been promised that the Messiah should be born of their race, because he was expected by the Hebrew people, foretold by the Peophets who were Hebrews, and his advent, his acts, his passion, death and resurrection were prefigured in the sacrifice, worship and ceremonials of the Hebrew law.

51. But, saving always the reverence due to the Holy Fathers and other Doctors, that explanation does not seem quite satisfactory. For it is an article of belief that the Church of the Faithful has been the only one in existence from the beginning of the world, and will thus endure to the end of time. The head of that Church is Jesus Christ, the mediator between God and men, by whose contemplation all things were made and created. Indeed, the faith in the Divine Trinity, though less explicitly, and the Incarnation of Word were revealed to the first man, and by him taught his children, who, in their turn, taught them their descendants. And thus, although most men have strayed into idolatry and deserted the true faith, many kept the faith they have received from their fathers, and observing the law of nature, stayed in the true Church of the Faithful, as is noticed by Cardinal Tolet in reference to Job, who was a saint among idolatrous Gentiles. And, although God had conferred special favors upon the Hebrew people, prescribed for them peculiar laws and ceremonials, and separated them from the Gentiles, yet those laws were not obligatory on the Gentiles, and the faithful Hebrews did not constitute a Church different from that of the Gentiles who professed their faith in one God and the coming of the Messiah.

52. All in all, it becomes clear that the Gentiles, also, belonged, like the Jew, to the fold of Christ, that is, to the same Church of the Faithful. It cannot, therefore, be correctly said that the words of Christ: "Other sheep I have, which are not of this fold," are applicable to the Gentiles, who had, in common with the Hebrews, the faith in God, the hope, prophecy, expectation, prodigies and preaching of the Messiah.

53. I, therefore, say that by the words *other sheep* may very

THE DIVINE MYSTERY. 77

well be understood those rational creatures, or animals, of whom we have been treating hitherto. They being, as we have said, capable of beatitude, and Jesus Christ being the moderator between God and man, as also every rational creature (for rational creatures attain to beatitude in consideration of the merits of Christ, through the grace he conferred upon them, without which beatitude is impossible of attainment,) every rational creature must have cherished, at the same time as the faith in God, the hope of the advent of Christ, and have had the revelation of his nativity in the flesh and of the principles of the law of grace. Those were, therefore, the sheep which were "not of human fold," and which Christ had to bring; the sheep which were to hear his voice, that is, the announcement of his advent and of the evangelical doctrine, either directly through him or through the Apostles; the sheep which, partaking with men of heavenly beatitude, were to realize "one fold and one shepherd."

54. To this interpretation, which I hold to be in no way improper, force is added by what we related, according to St. Hieronymus, of that little man who requested St. Anthony to pray for him and his fellows, unto the common God, whom he knew to have suffered in human flesh. For it implies that they were aware of the advent and of the death of Christ, whom, as God, they were anxious to propitiate, since sought, to that effect, the intercession of St. Anthony.

What we have hitherto deduced, accordingly solves the question as to how a woman can be got with child by an Incubus (Elemental.) In fact, it cannot be brought about by the vita assumed from man, agreeably to the common opinion which we confuted. It follows, therefore, that she is directly impregnated by the vita of the Incubus, which, being an animal and capable of giving life, has the vita of his own. And thus is fully explained the begetting of Giants from the intercourse of the Sons of God with the Daughters of men; for that intercourse gave birth to Giants who, although like unto men, were of higher stature, and, though begotten of Demons, and consequently of great strength, yet equalled them neither in might

nor in power.

55. In confirmation of the above inference, we observe that animals sprung from the mixing of different kinds do not breed, but are barren, as seen in certain kinds.

Now, we do not read of Giants having been begotten of other Giants, but of their having been born of the Sons of God, that is Elemental, and the Daughters of men. Being thus begotten of the vita of the Elemental mixed with the human vita, and being, as it were, an intermediate species between them and man, they had no generative power.

56. It will be retorted that, if the generation of Giants had really come from the combined vita of Incubi and women, Giants would still be born in our time, since there is no lack of women who have intercourse with Incubi, as shown by the Acts of St. Bernard and Peter of Alcantra.

57. Now, it must be observed that, after the flood, the air, which surrounds our earthly and aqeous globe, became, from the damp of the waters, thicker than it had been heretofore; and damp being the principle of curruption, that may be the reason why men do not live as they did before the flood. It is also on account of that thickness of the air that ethereal and igneons Demons, more corpulent than the others, can no longer dwell in the thick atmosphere, and if they do descend into it occasionally, do so only by force, much as divers descend into the depths of the sea.

58. Before the flood, when the air was not yet so thick, Demons came upon the earth and had intercourse with women. Thus procreating Giants whose stature was nearly equal to that of the Demons, their fathers. But now it is not so. The Incubi who approach women are equeous and of small stature. That is why they appear in the shape of little men, and, being aqueous, they are more lecherous. Poets have depicted Venus as born of the sea, in order to show, as explained by mythologists, that lust takes its source from damp. When, therefore, Demons of short stature impregnate women nowadays, the children that are born are not Giants, but men of ordinary size. It should, however, be known that when Demons have inter-

THE DIVINE MYSTERY. 81

course with women in their own natural body, without having resourse to any disguise or artifice, the women do not see them, or, if they do, see but an almost doubtful, barely invisible, shadow. But when they want to be be seen they assume a visible disguise and a palpable body. By what means this is effected is their secret, which our shortsighted philosophy is unable to discover. The only thing we know is that such disguise of body could not consist merely in concrete air, since this must take place through condensation, and, therefore, by the influence of cold. A body thus formed would feel cold like ice.

There is error in this, because it is *not* true that only the Elementals, that are aqueous, can have intercourse with earth people. The *one* reason why the Salamanders, or Elementals of Fire, which were really the Giants, or Sons of God, do not appear more often is because they are but few, and these few come only when some leader of the people is required. It is not the air or dampness which prevents them from reaching the earth plane, but the fact that there are few vessels properly fitted for the Great Work. All those who have truly learned the Æth Mystery can know these Salamanders, although not all can come into direct touch with them.

The world does not need Giants, and thus no Giants would be born, for the law of Hermes is: "As above so below." The demand for Giants is no longer, and, therefore, such would not be born, unless we understand it as Mental, Moral, or Spiritual Giants.

The means the Elementals use in order to become visible is now know as materialization. However, even this they need not employ, since those who want to see them, and do see them, are usually such as are Spiritually Developed, or, as the author would have it, such as have the perception of *Intuition*.

59. As for intercourse with an Incubus, wherein is to be found no element, not even the least, of an offence against Religion, it is hard to discover a reason why it should be more grevious

THE DIVINE MYSTERY. 83

than any other. Beastiality is a sin, because it degrades man, both body and soul, but when with Incubus it is quite the reverse. For the Incubus, by reason of his rational and immortal spirit, is equal to man; and by reason of his body more noble, because more subtile, he is more perfect and more dignified than man. Consequently, when having intercourse with an Incubus, man does not degrade, but rather dignifies his nature.

Beloved student, you may question why the writings of a Catholic are thus brought prominently to the fore. The reasons are many. Among these is the fact that many students of the mysterious consider that only the Occultist and Mystic, who is considered slightly weak anyhow by the people, has believed in these things. Herein it is shown, without danger of contradiction, that all the Church Fathers, even the Councils, have believed in this very thing.

Another reason is that it strengthens my contention that the Immaculate Conception is not only possible but that it is an *absolute* fact.

Still another reason is, that by quoting the Church itself on these points, there is no danger of my challenge ever being accepted, for to do so would overthrow the very foundation of religion. The work has, therefore, served its purpose, and served it well.

The student will bear in mind that all the paragraphs numbered appear in the original book, known as "Demoniality; or, Incubi and Succubi," by the Rev. Father Sinistrari of Ameno, (17th century,) although many had to be changed on account of the plain language used. All other parts are original, and for which the present publisher is responsible.

A number of entirely new Laws are given, and I challenge the entire world for a successful contradiction of them.

Furthermore, it would seem that the desire of the Elementals is to come into contact with mankind for the purpose of intercourse, and Immortality through that. Let me tell you frankly that such is *not* the case. All that these Elementals desire is to

THE DIVINE MYSTERY. 85

come into contact with true humanity and be *loved* by such, for they can become Immortal through this love just as well as through the intercourse, if not more easily so, since intercourse may lead to degradation. All that these Beautiful Beings desire is the *love* of those with whom they come into contact. They actually do not seek any other intercourse, but, like all women of the earth plane, they would not refuse the one whom they thus love.

It may be questioned whether, to my personal and absolute knowledge these things are facts, I answer, they *are absolutely* true in every respect. I know of those who, being Initiates of the Æth Brotherhood, have been able to save hundreds of these Beautiful Elementals. On the other hand, I know of many who have been the victims of disembodied Vampires. I have had both men and women to come to me from nearly every part of our country and plead with me to help them get rid of these deadly Vampires who were sapping their very life by sapping them of their vitality. In every case I have been successful. Thus do I know that these things are absolute facts, and, through the following of these Laws for many years, without failure in any case, I know that they are *absolute*.

The student will excuse me for making these personal remarks, but they are required in order to show that the things set forth are true.

THE SECRET INSTRUCTIONS.

The Elements.
Elementary Worlds.
The First Steps.
Our Guardian Angels.
Invocations.
Magical Invocation.
Man's Lost Kingdom.
Time of Invocation.
Daily Exercise.
The Three Breaths.
The Omnific Word and
Sacrifices.

CLYMER'S LAWS.

All Rights Reserved.

The Secret Instructions.

THE ELEMENTS.

The Ancient Masters recognized four original elements, which they called Fire, Water, Earth and Air. The ruling powers of these elements are known as Elementals. There has been a misunderstanding concerning these beings by even some of the best of scholars, and they have been mixed up with the Elementaries.

The Elementaries are those beings which man creates by a thought.

The Elementals are the beings of the elements.

For instance, the Gnomes are the spirits or messengers of Earth.

In modern times Paracelsus gave this name to these entities, and he did this because he found them to be true Etheric knowers. However, it must be borne in mind that they can only know the things which concern their own elements—the elements of Earth.

The Gnomes, as well as the spirits of the other elements, will become the true friends of men, if they are treated right. However, they will, as a rule, not give the secret of the precious metals to mankind unless under certain circumstances. Under some circumstances they will become the most bitter enemies of mankind.

THE DIVINE MYSTERY.

THE ELEMANTARY WORLD.

The sub-mineral, the mineral, the vegetable, and the animal worlds, are each presided over by a great created intelligence. Each dominion, or world, is peopled with unnumbered beings. Those of the sub-mineral are known as Sylphs; those of the mineral, Gnomes; those of the vegetable, Undines; and those of the animal, Salamanders.

Further, and in its most powerful aspect, the Gnomes are the spirits of the earth, the Salamanders the spirits of fire, the Sylphs the spirits of air, and the Undines the spirits of water.

Gob is the King of the Gnomes, and is usually in a dread form; the fierce and terrible Djin is the King of the Salamanders; the graceful Paralda, Queen of the Sylphs; and the beautiful although fateful Nicksa, Queen of the Undines.

The last two, Paralda, Queen of the Sylphs, and Nicksa, Queen of the Undines, are the most friendly to man. The first two are the most potent, but the most difficult to control.

The *Great Law* concerning these Beings is: "If thou wouldst be loved by fairy queens, by Sylphs and Undines, and the beautiful damsals of light, be chaste as the moon toward earthly women; for the elemental spirits are ofttimes jealous of the daughters of men."—*Magical Axiom.*

The throne of Paralda, Queen of Sylphs, is to the East; of Gob, of the Gnomes, to the North; of Nicksa, of the Undines, to the West; and of Djin, of the Salamanders, to the South.

The Occult or Magical Master has dominion over all these Sovereigns of Nature, and, under fixed laws, can direct their especial forces for the good of the human race.

THE FIRST STEP.

It is, first of all, necessary to purify the heart by Faith, and the greatest Axiom of the Occult or Magical Master is:

"*Go forward and Faith will come to you.*"

Thus D'Lembert remarked to some one who complained of the cloud which certain demonstrations had left in his understanding.

THE DIVINE MYSTERY.

He who doubts is condemned to failure, but if he holds to the one idea he will succeed, for, as he goes forward, so will faith come to him. Here will we meet with the Potent Law, so ably given by Tennyson, in "Vivian:"

> "And since he kept his mind on one sole aim,
> Nor ever touch fierce wine, nor tasted flesh,
> Nor owned a sensual wish, to him the wall
> That sunders ghosts and shadow-casting men
> Became a crystal, and he saw them thro' it,
> And heard their voices talk behind the wall,
> And learned their elemental secrets,
> Powers and forces."

This is the great law, and the sooner the student will learn to understand the sooner he can become Master.

He who enters into the natural way of holy living, may see the Silence of his Soul absolutely certain of success. He can then command in Love, and it shall be. He can then call upon the popentates of the East to purify the air, and it shall be; and thus with all things. The Elementals of Fire, Sylphs and Undines are best controlled through Love, as that is their desire, but they may be commanded by mere Force, but this is not advisable.

OUR GUARDIAN ANGELS.

The spirits of the various divisions of time are the guardians of everything evolved or born. But a special Intelligence is ordained to accompany every person, and is known as the Personal Guardian, who acts in conjunction with the Zodiacal and Planetary Angels. It is for this reason that Talismans and Amulets, made properly under certain signs, must have a certain influence upon the wearer, and draw nigh the Planetary Spirits and cause them to give their help.

The Personal Guardian never, for a moment, leaves the Soul. It is the adviser of the Soul, and it acts through what is known to the true Occultist and Mystic as the "Still Small Voice Within."

The four great steps which all Neophytes must know and

understand are.
To Know.
To Will.
To Dare.
To Keep Silent.

This embraces: First, knowledge of the ways and means to accomplish; second, the intention to perform; third, the courage to execute; and, lastly, in *Silence* is typified not the mere habitual absence of expression, not alone the concealing of dangerous secrets from the unworthy, but, also, the complete shutting out of all extraneous things that would interfere with the purpose and intent of the operation, and especially the refraining from all boasting as to results. Silence is, in fact, a cardinal principle with the true Philosopher, and is enjoined by all schools. It is a known fact that all magicians who have boasted of their works have come to violent deaths.—Dr. Zell.

The reason that men do not consciously recognize their Guardian Angels, is that they have misused their power of dominion and have become tyrants, destroying in the most relentless manner the creatures of the four inferior worlds—those ruled by the Sylph, whose potentate is Paralda; that of the Gnomes, which is ruled by the potentate Gob; that of the Undines, whose potentate is Nicksa; and that or the Salamanders, whose King is Djin.

Because of this destruction by man, all the kingdoms of nature have combined against man, and each world has thrown into his body such material that his sensitiveness has been greatly impaired, and man must retrace his steps and recognize the right of every living creature before he can again come into communication with those Forces, and see and hear the mysteries that they have to unfold. Every particle of cruelty and animosity, as well as self-righteousness and self-sufficiency, must be eliminated from the personality before one can hope to secure the services of these beings of the four worlds.*

---

* The student should read "The Irreconcilable Gnome."—La Petit Albert.

INVOCATION.

When once the Neophyte has freed himself from cruelty, and has in his or her soul an all-consuming love for the handiwork of God, he may, by appropriate means, evoke the creatures of the elementary worlds, and they will at once break the chains that bind him, and help him in every way possible.

This can also be accomplished without this Love; by force of the Invocation, but this is extremely dangerous, and these very forces will destroy such.

It is by far best to rule through love, for

"Love rules the court, the camp, the grove,
And men below and saints above,
For love is *heaven and heaven is love.*"
—Scott.

MAGICAL INVOCATION.

"Learn thyself to triumph over fear by wisdom, and spirits will come down out of heaven to serve thee. I, Solomon, thy father, King of Israel and Palmyra, have sought and obtained for my portion the holy Chocmah, which is the wisdom of Adonai. And I have become the king of spirits, both of heaven and earth, the Masters of the powers of the air and the living souls of the seas, because I possess the key of the Secret Gates of Light."

Secret Clavicle of Solomon, addressed to his son Rehoboam.

"The art of magic is the art of employing Invisible, or so-called Spiritual agencies, to obtain visible results."—Hartmann.

Carry into the Silence of the Soul the consecrated Hexagram, the Seal of Solomon and King, and the Magic Wand*. The body must be cleansed through purification. The operator must then look to the east, and point thither with the Wand, breathe freely seven times, and in a clear voice say:

"In the name of the Sacred Tetragrammation, I invoke thee, Paralda."

---

* See the "Grand Grimore" for full instruction for making Wand.

Then turning to the north, and pointing thither with the Wand, and breathing seven times, say:

"In the name of the Sacred Tetregrammation, I invoke thee, Gob."

Then turning to the west, and pointing thither with the Wand, and breathing seven times, say:

"In the name of the Sacred Tetregrammation, I invoke thee, Nicksa."

Then turning to the south, and pointing thither with the Wand, and breathing seven times, say:

"In the name of the Sacred Tetregrammation, I invoke thee, Djin."

Then turning to the east, and, looking upward, complete the Invocation by saying:

"Let the Holy Breath penetrate every fibre of my body, and cleanse me. Let the living Mercury of earth touch every resistant molecule in my body, dissolving it and cleansing me. Let the Waters of Life flow through every nerve and artery of my body, and cleanse me. Let the burning Fire of God consume all dross of my body. Then shall I be worthy to stand in the presence of the Masters."

During the entire time of this Invocation the Hexagram should be suspended directly over head.

After the Invocation it is necessary to dismiss the Elementals, and this should be done in a manner that will help them:—

"May the peace and love of God, our Father, ever be with you, and may it be His will that one and all may reach that Immortality of the Soul which all desire."

MAN'S LOST KINGDOM.

Man has lost his knowledge by cruelty to the four orders of the inferior Intelligences. Because of his cruelty all nature has arrayed itself against him, and all entities have joined in the destruction of man's sensitized state. To be restored, love must take the place of this cruelty and hate, and by determined effort this may be speedily accomplished. Love is the Key to Redemption, as it is to Regeneration and Immortality.

THE DIVINE MYSTERY.

Let your motto be: Let love to all creatures, in the lower and in the higher heavens, be the emblem of my soul. May I be able to transmute all hate, bigotism and self-righteousness into that love which the Gods would want me have.

TIME OF INVOCATION.

The Invocation to the Elementals should always be observed at 6 o'clock in the morning, 12 noon, and 6 in the evening. At midnight under special circumstances.

DAILY EXERCISES.

The Three Breaths, or Three Beatitudes.

First. The Inspiration of God in all His characteristics and attributes. A full deep breath filling all parts of the body. The *thought* is of vast importance.

Second. Breath of Discrimination, or of drawing in the spiritual ether or Æth from the ordinary air. Take a deep full inspiration, expire in short puffs, keeping or holding in mind continually the thought or prayer, "I will to become (whatever the desire may be, but such desire must be one that is pure and holy.)"

Third. Breath of Exaltation, Aspiration, reaching up, holding in thought the highest possible spiritual ideal.

These exercises should be followed morning, noon and night.

The Invocation to the Elementals should be followed every day.

THE OMNIFIC WORD.

Love is really the Omnific Word. It is the Lost Word of which so much has been said; but this word cannot be pronounced. In fact, it could never be pronounced. The Word must be made flesh, that is, it must become personified in the one who would use it. It must be developed in the soul; it then becomes a Word of mighty power.

Love is a Talisman. It is Omnific. It will control all the influences of Paralda, Gob, Nicksa and Djin. It can cure all manner of diseases, cast out demons, and even raise the dead.

SACRIFICES.

In order to be most successful in this great work, sacrifices

THE DIVINE MYSTERY.

are necessary, but these are not to be of the old dispensation type, not sacrifices of blood, but of love.

The sacrifice to nature. There is a law of equivalents—that we must give to whatever gives to us. Nature gives to us our bodies, and we are in debt to nature for them. There is a great personality called Diva, and known as the God of Nature. Under this Diva are the potentates of Fire, of Earth, of Water and of Air, whose names, as you have been taught, are Djin, Gob, Nicksa and Paralda.

We must pay homage to the great potentiality, Diva, if we wish to invoke these potentates.

An ancient article reads thus: "Angi (fire) is the mouth of the Gods," and the ancient world believed in the necessity of this sacrifice. So they instituted the Sacrificial Altar, or the altar of burnt offerings, and they burned all manner of things thereon. This was a sacrifice incident to the childhood of the race, which we have outgrown, and we now repay Nature for all her benefits by helping her to provide for her children.

The Second Sacrifice.—This is the Sacrifice of Knowledge. She gave us much, and we must offer her the best we have—the best time for study and research.

The Third Sacrifice.—This is to Humanity. The race must be represented by particular persons. We must seek and find such as need, and note the willingness with which we give, and know that even a cup of water given to a famishing one is for the race.

The Fourth Sacrifice.—This is to the world below the human—to the birds, animals, and other living things. Kindness and consideration for them is considered as a sacrifice. No day should pass that we do not spread some little food upon the ground somewhere for something living. It is natural that those living in the country, where Nature is at her best, should have the greatest opportunities, but all can do something.

THE HUMAN SOUL BEFORE BIRTH AND AFTER DEATH.

Constitution of Man and the Universe.
Key of the Gospels.
Gospel Initiation.
ACCORDING TO PISTIS SOPHIA.

From the Coptic (Egyptian)
Manuscript of Pistis Sophia,
BY M. E. AMELINEAU.

The Manuscript here used is that owned by
Frank Oscar Biberstein, 38△,
And no doubt the only one owned in
America.

The Imperialistic Council is indebted to Brother Biberstein for the privilege of allowing this valuable work to be placed before the Members of the Order. This old manuscript of the Coptic Christians is in perfect harmony with the Doctrines set forth concerning the Elementals.

Analysis of Pistis Sophia.

 **BY**
M. E. AMELINEAU.

As in all known Gnostic works, and we have knowledge of at least four of them, the revelation of the wonderful Gnosis, the knowledge of which places the happy possessor in a position infinitely advantageous to obtain eternal happiness after death is put in the mouth of Jesus, resuscitated from among the dead.

The author of Pistis Sophia assures us that after His resurrection, Jesus passed seven years in teaching his admirable Gnosis to His Disciples, and to the company of men and women who had followed Him.

When the first scene of the book opens, Jesus is seated on the Mount of Olives with all those who surround Him, the twelve Apostles, Mary His mother, Mary Magdalen, Martha and Salome. (These are at least the principal actors, who speak one after another, as the initiation is unfolded.)

Hardly have we settled on the place where the following scenes are to take place, when Jesus, seated a little apart from His Disciples, is surrounded with a great light which serves Him as a vestment, and transports Him to the heavens in the midst of the freight of the cosmic elements. His Disciples are in a state of astonishment and stuperfaction at the sight of the light which has taken Jesus away. They make their prayers heard, and Jesus comes back to them to explain the mysteries that He can and must explain to them. He explains to them at first

that He has gone towards His Father; that the vestment of light that was brought to Him on the Mount of Olives was the very same that He laid down in one of the Eons when He descended on the earth. He begins then to explain to them certain words of the Gospel and certain acts preparatory to His descent on the earth, as the coming of Elias in the person to John and the annunciation of Gabriel to Mary, the election of the Apostles in consequence of putting superior souls into their bodies at the moment of conception.

Then, all at once, and without any transition, and, one must almost say, without the least detail of the book indicating any break, He tells of His ascent into the Superior Mysteries of the Eons. In these different mysteries of the different Enos, the chiefs, or archons, of each place, the guardians of the gates and all the inhabitants of the Eons crossed, made way at His presence, astonished, stupefied, overcome, constrained by the magic words with which the garment of light which is upon Jesus is covered.

But Jesus in some of these Eons (and there again is a break in the continuity of the recital without there being any break in the text) only retires after punishment on a certain number of their inhabitants. The archons, indeed, at sight of Him, wished to fight the light which clothed Him. They were punished for it by the taking away of a third of their light which was found in them, by the changing of the revolution of their spheres, which turned them to the left in place of turning to the right, which threw the greatest confusion into the horoscopes which skillful men were drawing on earth, and caused them great confusion since they knew not of this change, and calculated as if the astral movement were continuous, while during six months it was to the left and during six months to the right. But this did not prevent their work from being right when the movement corresponded to the original motion which took place during half of the year.

By a change of subject sudden enough, Jesus, at a question from Mary Magdalen, explained to her how souls would have been able to wait in the Eon in question until the number of

THE DIVINE MYSTERY.

perfect souls should be filled; then how these souls had been created, how they had shared the fate of the spheres whose revolution had been changed inversely, and then Jesus took up a continuation of the first subject of which He had spoken. It was then that Pistis Sophia appears, whose misfortunes and whose safety will be related at length in the work.

This Pistis Sophia was one of the twenty-four superior emanations. Looking up one day she saw the Light in the "firmament of the Grand Treasury of Light." She wished to reach the place, and ceased to practice the mystery of the place which she inhabited. She sang a hymn to the light which she had seen. But in place of being heard, she knew that she had only drawn the jealously and hatred of those who shared her dwelling. They pursued her. She fled beyond her Eon, fell into the depths of Shadowy Chaos, and there found herself the object of all the attacks of the archons of this chaos and of those who are found beneath it. These archons, created by emanation a crowd of strange beings, whose mission it was to take from Pistis Sophia the luminous part which belonged to her. She was then plunged into all the horrors of the shades, and was the object of all the attacks of the diverse and horrible emanations created to fight her. But, if her trials were great, her courage was still greater. She did not lose her confidence at all. She turned to the light and addressed to it a hymn of repentance, or "a repentance," as the text expresses it. This repentance, like the twelve following, is based on the Psalms suited to the different states through which she passes, and, in order to make the thing clearer, the Disciples, men and women gave the explanation of it, reciting just the Psalm from which the repentance was copied. At the ninth repentance Sophia is heard. Jesus, the Savior, is sent to her, and draws her by degrees from the miserable state where she is, then finally saves her from chaos. The repentances are then changed to thanksgivings. Jesus leads her below the thirteenth Eon, and leaves her there, charging her to call Him when the time should come when certain archons would desire to maltreat her. This time comes when Jesus is in the world of men on the Mount of

THE DIVINE MYSTERY. 113

Olives. Jesus went, then, to her aid as He had promised, and leads her into the thirteenth Eon. Meanwhile, after the thirteenth repentance of Pistis Sophia, and in the midst of the explanation of her first hymn of thanksgiving, the text is all at once interrupted by a page inserted, on the left hand page of folio 114, which contains a theme altogether different from those we have found up to this time. Then the folio 115, on the right hand page, is this title: "Second Volume of Pistis Sophia," and this second volume opens by the continuation of the preceding explanation, that is to say, the explanations of the first hymn of thanksgiving uttered by Pistis Sophia.

After Pistis Sophia has been reinstated in her Eon, the book changes its style; that is to say, questions, which up to this point, have been found only at times, become the general rule from this time forward.

These questions relate at first to certain particular points of the constitution of the invisible worlds; then they turn almost entirely on eschatological problems, and the different questions to which they give rise, for different categories of souls. I will not devote myself to analyzing them here. The reader will find them all at length in the work which I have translated. That which will suffice now is to show that safety after death will correspond to the degree of initiation received by souls; that sinning souls not initiated may be saved by the faithful; that sinning and initiated souls are condemned to be lost irrevokably, and nothing can save them.

I should add here that one of the chief features of the Valentinian eschatology in the Pistis Sophia is the possibility of amending a former evil life by a second better one, for the disciples of Valentine and Valentine himself accepted absolutely the doctrine of transmigration of souls.

Here, again, the explanations which Jesus gives His Disciples are all at once interrupted by a title thrown right into the midst of their unfolding. (A part of the books of the Savior.) The passage thus announced comprises two leaves. It does not concern, closely or remotely, that which precedes or that which follows, and the third leaf after this title is a continuation of

THE DIVINE MYSTERY. 115

the seemingly so inappropriately interrupted explanations. These explanations continue by the examination of new questions, which the Disciples raise in the eschatological ethics of Valentinism. These give Jesus an opportunity to describe certain particulars of the Valentenian Inferno up to the moment when a new direction of the work is announced by the title: "Extracts from the Books of the Savior." This part is no more finished, it seems to me, than the others. It is Mary Magdalene who speaks in the last lines, and her sentence does not seem to be complete.

With the "Extract from the Book of the Savior," I have just said, the Gnostic work takes a new turn. The opening part shows that it is entirely a new book that we have here, for it commences with these words: "It came to pass, then, that after they had crucified our Lord, that the third day He rose from among the dead." As in other books, as I have already shown, the Disciples gathered near the Savior, on the borders of the Sea, and address a prayer to Him, to which Jesus responded, explaining to them the position of the planets after having placed them at His right hand. These planets are five in number—Saturn, Mars, Mercury, Venus and Jupiter. They are governed by the last, in which is placed Sabaoth, the little and the good. Then on the question of Mary Magdalene, what are the paths of the Midst, which are five in number, each of which has for its governor archons, whose names are given, names as strange as the forms of these archons? Then Jesus sends away the powers of the left to the place that they should occupy. Urged again by His Disciples, He replies to them that He was to confer on them the Baptism for the Remission of Sins, and, in fact He does confer it on them. After having thus conferred this Baptism, Jesus said to His Disciples that there are other Baptisms, and He undertook their explation.

The real conclusion of the work is found shortened, I believe, in a page which is attached to the end of the manuscript. It speaks of the dispersion of the Apostles, three by three, towards the cardinal points, to preach the good news of the Gnostic Gospel. Christ confirming their preaching by signs and won-

ders, in such a way that the whole earth might know the Kingdom of God.

CHAPTER II.
The Universe.

The Pleroma, or Universe, physical and super-physical, is composed of three worlds, of three planes which interpenetrate each other, and which are separated in the illustrations to facilitate the description.

The higher, or Celestial plane, is formed, according to the author of Pistis Sophia, of twenty-four concentric circles which he calls the twenty-four mysteries. They correspond to the twenty-four elders of the Apocalypse, and have for key the twenty-four jewels which adorn the mystic name Yod-He-Vau-He. (See on this subject the works of Eliphas Levi.)

The twenty-fourth mystery is most closely in touch with the lower worlds, and the first mystery is the most central. It is the first mystery which Jesus will describe in detail, and it is that which includes the heritage of the Elect, as well as the Force Principles, or celestial creatures.

The middle plane, or astral plane of the Kabbala, is represented by the dragon of Hermetism (ouroboros) of the Initiates, which forms a circle, since the mouth devours the tail. This dragon symbolizes the billows of fire of the astral plane, the sea of flames of Hemetic Initiation, and the pergatory of Christians.

The dragon is divided into twelve parts, or Eons. Each of these Eons has a door which opens towards the superior world, "towards the Heights," says the text. Each of these doors is concealed on the inside by a veil, and is guarded on the outside by an astral spirit, or archon, who is called the Ruler of the Door (or gate) of the Heights. These twelve Eons correspond to the twelve houses of the astrological zodiac. They serve as a place of trial for condemned souls, who enter into the different Eons through the mouth of the dragon (entrance of condemned souls.)

The physical plane, or plane of corporal humanity, is sur-

rounded on all sides by the astral dragon. No being then will be able to come from heaven on the material plane or go from the material plane into heaven without having crossed this domain of the dragon, this world of archons, filled with torments and snares. The physical plain begins at the circle of the firmament, situated within the circle of chaos, and this physical plane includes the stars and the luminaries, or planets, and at the center of the world of humanity.

In the narrative of Valentine, these three planes enclose one another, from the world of humanity at the center, to the first mystery at the periphery, and the celestial world goes even farther, with intermediaries between the different planes.

If we had followed the illustration exactly, it would be well nigh impossible to understand the construction of the first mystery and its relations with the rest of the Universe, or Pleroma. That is why, in our general illustration, we have drawn the celestial plane apart from and above the two others, although normally it should envelop them. Between the celestial plane and the astral plane there is a place of transition, the thirteenth Eon, and the astral plane is still another plane of transition where Pistis Sophia was led. Finally, between the astral plane and the physical plane exist diverse spheres (sphere of destiny or second sphere, spere of chaos or first sphere), which indicates the planes of progressive materializalion of the Divine Force.

He who reads the following translation will be struck with the duties of the secondary agencies, named Receivers. There are the Receivers of Light, or the Peaceful Receivers, and the Receivers of Darkness. The part of these agents is to go to seek for souls at the moment when they are to leave the body, to conduct them across Creation during three days, and then to put them into the hands of those who must award or punish them.

The Messenger of Death.

Ancient Egypt believed in a messenger of Death who came to look for the soul at a fixed moment, and a work on Ethics, attributed to the Scribe Khonson-Hotep, tells us of it in a maxim, which I shall quote here:

"Place before thyself, as thy object to attain, an old age worthy of testimony that thou mayst be found to have perfected thy house, which is in the funeral valley, on the morning of the hiding away of thy body. So when, for thee, the Messenger of Death shall come to take thee let him find one who is ready."

However, an examination of the illustration, especially of that of the Pleroma, will enable one to find in the mind this arrangement of the worlds and dissipate all difficulties.

Let us say, now, something of the inhabitants of these different worlds.

The Inhabitants of the Invisible World.

The world of humanity is inhabited by souls clothed with bodies. Though invisible beings, everywhere we shall find there above all the Pacific Receivers, appointed to receive the soul on its going forth from the body, and to carry it as far as the astral plane, where it will find a crowd of beings with whom it may have to do.

These beings of the astral plane are chiefly the receivers of the archons, the archons of destiny, and the archons in all their offices. The archons are especially enemies of the human soul and they are particularly hostile to it when initiation does not permit it to defend itself.

The Celestial Plane.

The celestial plane shows us at first the Receivers of Light, the Receivers of the middle plane, then a crowd of mysterious beings, classed in three great centres—the middle, the right and left. This right and left are those not of the illustration, but of the Christ of Glory, who occupies the center of the figure.

In the middle we find the Virgin of Light, appointed to seal souls according to their exaltation. Then Iao, the great Supreme One; then the Twelve Deacons, the seven Virgins of Light, with the Receivers, the Deacons and the Angels of the midst.

At the left we find the only door by which heaven communicates with the other worlds. This door unites thirteenth Eon with the Treasury of Light, whence have come most of the

emanations which adorn the celestial plane. It is, indeed, from this Treasury of Light that have emanated the nine guardians and the Savior of the twins (Jumeau), which are at the left of Christ, and the five trees, and the three amens, and the seven voices which are at His right.

The five trees have sent forth, in their turn, each a creative Light.

The light of the first tree has emanated Ieou.

The light of the second tree has emanated the guardians of the veil of the great light.

The light of the third tree has emanated Melchizedec.

The light of the fourth tree and fifth tree has emanated the Two Prohegomenes.

Finally, if we say that Ieou has emanated, in his turn, Sabaoth the Good, He whom Jesus calls His Heavenly Father, one will have a complete idea of the emanations which constitute the celestial plane, which our illustration makes clear enough.

CHAPTER III.

Man—Constitution of Man.

The ideas already furnished will make it easy for the reader to understand the origin of the different principles which constitute man incarnate.

Composition of the Human Being.

The human being, as he presents himself to us on the earth, is thus composed:

1. A hylic, or corporal body.
2. An intermediary principal; the spirit of spiritual imitation.
3. The immortal soul.

To these principles it is necessary to add the forces not incarnated, which are:

A. The heavenly principle.
B. Destiny.

The physical body comes from the earth, and returns to it. It is shaped by the immediately superior principle.

The Spirit of Spiritual Imitation plays an important part in

the work of Valentine. It is the prinriple of attraction downward. The origin of the satanic impulses, which draw the soul to the enjoyment of matter.

The more the soul follows the impulses of this principle of evil, the more powerful will be the bond which unites her to it, and the greater will be the difficulty she will have in escaping from the torments into which the Spirit of Spiritual Imitation will lead her. This spirit, which comes from the sphere of Destiny, and which must remain there if the soul succeeds in breaking the bond which attaches her to it.

The reader will observe, also, in reading the eschatological part of Pistis Sophia, that there is often a reference to one part of the human being named the Spirit of Spiritual Imitation, in such a way that the doctrine of Valentine—man is composed of the body, of spiritual imitation, of the soul, until the soul becomes spiritual and blessed.

The spiritual imitation has the form of the body; is born with the body; is attached to it during life, and follows it even to death; witness of all the actions of the body and of the soul; accusing the later after death and leading her to sin during life.

So, with the ancient Egyptians, man was composed of the body, of the double, of the soul, which becomes blest, or spiritual after death, if she has been found just in the supreme judgment of Osiris. It is to the double that spiritual imitation corresponds. The double was a thin image of the body, an imitation, more tenuous, more spiritual in every way, which was born with the body, grew with the body, then reviving without the body in consequence of certain magic ceremonies, continued to live after death in the place where the body was preserved.

Spirit of Imitation.

Analysis of the Author of Pistis.

And the Spirit of Spiritual Imitation makes the soul yield, and forces her to do all sinful things, give way to all passions, commit all sins ceaselessly, and it remains opposed to the soul, and is her enemy, making her commit all these evils and all these sins. And it excites the peaceful "Liturges" to be its wit-

THE DIVINE MYSTERY.

ness in all the sins which it caused her to commit, and, even when she would repose in the night, it excites her with worldly desires. In a word, it devotes itself to all the works which the archons had ordered it to do, and becomes the enemy of the soul, and makes her do what she does not wish to do.

The Spirit of Spiritual Imitation, destiny and the body (the mystery of baptism) separate themselves into one part, the soul, also, and the essence separate themselves into another part. The mystery of baptism remains between the two.

But to this center of attraction downwards is opposed the celestial essence, center of attraction upwards to the high and the Divine, origin of the ideal on earth, of pure desire, and of regenerating sacrifice.

This celestial virtue comes directly from the Virgin of Light of the celestial plane. It returns there immediately after death, and remains attached during the whole of the terrestrial life to the soul, to enlighten it and allow it to elevate itself by comprehending Divine Love.*

The Immortal Soul, free to follow the impulses below or the ecstasies from above, is sent on earth to gain initiation. As long as it has not penetrated the principle of creation, it is obliged to return to incarnate again.

Destiny has no part in human substance. Unmoved spectator, it is there to stop the course of physical existence at the marked day, and, that done, it returns to the first sphere, whence it came.

The reader will understand, now, the following which recapitulates all this.

When the little child comes to earth, the Heavenly Essence is weak in it, the soul, also, is weak in it, the Imitation of the Spirit is feeble in it; in a word, the three are feeble together. No one knows what he will be, good or evil, and the body even is feeble, and the little child eats the nourishment of the world

---

* Theology has figured two principles. The Spirit of Imitation by the Angel of Darkness, and the Heavenly Essence by the Guardian Angel who helps every man in the world.

THE DIVINE MYSTERY.

of the archons, and the Essence from the archons draws to itself the part of the essence which is in the food, and the Soul draws to it that part of the soul which is in the food, and the Spirit of Spiritual Imitation draws to it the bad part which is in the nourishment with its desires, and the body also attracts to it the insensible matter which is in the food. As to Destiny, it takes nothing from the food, because it is not mingled with it.*

Little by little the Essence, the Soul, the Spirit of Imitation, attains its growth. Each becomes conscious according to its nature. The Essence desires to seek the light of the heights; the Soul, also, wishes to seek the place of justice, which is mixed, that is to say, that it is the place of mixture; the Spirit of Imitation seeks, also, all wickedness, all desires, and all sins; the body, itself, it desires nothing, but that it may get strength from matter.

Origin of the Soul.

The soul of ordinary men takes its first origin from the archons' own light; that is to say, from the chiefs who exercise their power in the sphere of Destiny. Thus we can understand the rage and anger of those archons when the human soul succeeds in crushing it's creators with all the superiority due to it's sufferings valiantly borne, and to it's personal initiation. Then the soul passes like a "track of fire" in the midst of the archons, who draw back full of fright in their powerless hatred. All that the archons possessed of the Divine, their light, their essence, the breath of their mouth even, became the substance of the human soul, while the tears of their eyes, the sweat of their bodies, became the principle of animal souls. The distribution of the Divine substance was regulated according to astrological aspects.

Such is the explanation of the follow magnificent quotation:

"And when the time of the number of Melchizedec, the Grand Receiver of Light, had come, he went into the midst of the

---

* Louis Michel de Figanieres has clearly developed the divers localization of the foods of men.

THE DIVINE MYSTERY. 131

Eons and of all the attendant archons, into the Sphere and into the Destiny, and he took away the shining splendors from all the archons of the Eons, and all the archons of Destiny, as well as those of the Sphere; for he took away from them that which troubled them, and he influenced the Lord, who was their chief, to make their arches to revolve quickly, and he took from them the essence which was in them, the breath of their mouth, the tears from their eyes, the sweat from their bodies; and Melchizedec, the Receiver of Light, purified all these virtues in order to carry their light to the Treasury of Light, while the *liturges* of the archons collected together with each other all their material parts, and the liturges of all the archons of Destiny, with the liturges of the Sphere, those which are under the Eons, took them in order to make of them the souls of men, of animals, of reptiles, or of beasts, or of birds, and to send them into this world of humanity.

"And, further, the receivers of the Sun and the receivers of the Moon, having looked at the heavens, and seen the shape of the progress of the Eons, and those of Destiny, and those of the Sphere, then they took from them the virtue of light, and the receivers prepared to leave it until they could give it to the receivers of Melchizedec, the purifiers of light; and their corporal residue they carried into the sphere which is below the Eons, in order to make of it, also, the souls of reptiles, or of animals, or of wild beasts, or of birds, according to the circle of the archons of that sphere, and according to all the forms of its revolution."

The Soul After Physical Death.

Leaving aside for the moment the part the soul plays during incarnation in this physical body, let us content ourselves with knowing that the end of this incarnation is to acquire *Initiation* and occupy ourselves with the important question of the evolution of the soul after death.

According to the Kabbala, the three principles of man go through evolution, attempting to regain their original place. The physical body returns to earth, the ætherial or astral body returns to the astral plane whence it came, and the immortal

spirit tries to return to the center of its celestial origin.

This doctrine will be made clear in a very remarkable way in the following pages. We shall see, indeed, that the soul of the Initiate returns to the heritage of light after having left successively, and in their place of respective origin, the Spirit of Spiritual Imitation and Destiny. When the soul has not been able to gain by initiation the knowledge of the symbols and passwords, which open the gates of the astral dragon of the terrible place of the Eons, then the Spirit of Imitation becomes its accuser and tormentor, and the black angel comes from the world of the angels of darkness, takes possession of its victim and tortures it. But this torture is never eternal.

The Soul of the Non-Repentant and Uninitated Sinner.

Phases of Post-Mortem Evolution in General.

Now, when the time of this kind of a man is accomplished, first Destiny comes. She causes the man to be led to his death by means of the archons, and there fetters those with whom they have been associated by Destiny, and then comes the Tranquilizing Receivers, in order to lead this soul out of the body.

And then the Tranqualizing Receivers spend three days making with this soul the round of all the places, leading it to all the Eons of the world, while Destiny and the Spirit of Spiritual Imitation follow, and the essence withdraws to the Virgin of Light.

And after three days, the Tranquilizing Receivers lead this soul below, to the Hell of Chaos, and, when they have lead it to the depth of Chaos, they deliver it to those who punish it, and the Receivers withdraw to their own place, according to the plan for the work of the archons in the going out of souls.

And the Spirit of Imitation becomes the receiver of the soul, and he contends with it, and puts it again into the torment on account of the sins which he has made it commit, and it is then at great emnity with the soul.

And when the soul has finished with the punishment for the sins which it has committed, the Spirit of Imitation makes it go

THE DIVINE MYSTERY. 135

forth from Chaos, fighting it and reproaching it at every step (or every place) for the sins it had committed, and he leads it on the road of the archons of the midst, and, when he has reached them, they introduce the soul into the mystery of Destiny, and if it does not meet (or find) them they seek their Destiny.

And those archons punish the soul both according to its sins and that which it merits.

And I will tell you the kind of their punishment in the emanation of the Pleroma.

If it happens then that the time of these punishments of this soul, in the judgments of the archons of the midst has been accomplished, the Spirit of Spiritual Imitation leads the soul out of all the places of the archons of the midst. He introduces it into the presence of the light of the sun, according to the order of the first man Ieou, and he places it near the judge; that is, the Virgin of Light. She tries this soul to see if she finds a sinning soul. She throws into it her virtue of light to keep it with the body and the union of the senses.

Concerning all that, I will tell you the type when I speak of the emanation of the Pleroma.

And the Virgin of Light seals this soul. She send with it one of her receivers, in order to place in a body suited to the sins which the soul has committed. And in truth I tell you this. She does not leave this soul in the various transformations of the body until it has paid the last century according to what it has deserved.

And of all that I will tell you of the type, as well as of the type of the body into which they have thrown according to the sins of such souls. All that I will tell you when I have finished telling you about the emanations from the Pleroma.

(The soul who has not listened to the Spirit of Spiritual Imitation in any of its works.)

Become good, it has received the mysteries of light, is in the second stage, or has received those of the third.

If the time of this soul has come to go out of the body, then the Spirit of Spiritual Imitation joins itself to this soul, as well

THE DIVINE MYSTERY. 137

as Destiny. He joins the soul on the way by which it will enter into the heights, and, before it has gone very far into the heights, it pronounces the mystery of the dissolution of the seals and of the bonds of the Spirit of Spiritual Imitation which the archons have attached to the soul, and when the mystery has been said the bonds of the Spirit of Spiritual Imitation are dissolved, and he leaves her, according to what has been said.

And immediately it becomee a great ray of shining light. It traverses all the places of the archons and all the hierarchies of the shades, until it arrives at the place of its own kingdom of which it has received the mystery.

The Revolution of the Soul of the Initiate

This soul is one who has received the mystery in the first exterior stage. If, after it has received the mysteries, and accomplished them, it returns and sins again after the accomplishment of the mysteries, and the time is not come when this soul must go out of the body, and in this hour the soul pronounces the mystery in order not to retain the Spirit of Spiritual Imitation and Destiny, or allow it to follow, but without the least power.

At this hour, the receivers of this soul with the mysteries that it has received arrived, they take this soul from the hands of the Pacifying Receivers, and the receivers withdraw into the works of the archons, according to the plan of the going out of souls. And then the receivers of this soul, those who belong to the light, become wings of light for this soul, and a vestment of light for her, and do not lead it into the Chaos because it is not permitted to introduce into Chaos a soul who has received the mysteries; but they put it on the road to the archons of the midst, and when she has come there to the archons of the midst, the archons come before this soul, in great fear and trouble, with different expressions, all in uncontrollable fear.

Then soul pronounces the mystery of their password, and they greatly fear, and fall on their faces, fearing in the presence of the mystery which she has pronounced and of the password, and this soul abandons them to their destiny, saying to them: "Take for yourselves your Destiny. I shall never come from

THE DIVINE MYSTERY. 139

this time forth into your place. I have become a stranger to you forever. I go to the place of my inheritance."

Then the soul will have finished speaking these words, the Receivers of Light will introduce her in the plane of Destiny, where she will give the password of this place and of the seals which I shall tell you of in speaking of the emanations of the Pleroma. And she will give the Spirit of Spiritual Imitation to the archons, and say to them the mystery of the bonds with which they have attached her, and she will say to them: "Take for yourselves your Spirit of Imitation (spiritual). I shall henceforth come into your place no more forever." And she will give to each one the seal and password. And when the soul will have finished saying these words, the Receivers of Light will fly with her into the heights, and lead her into all the Eons. She will give to each her password and the password of all the places, the seals and the tyrants of King Adamas (Thirteenth Eon) she gives the password of all the archons of all the places of the left. And the Receivers will lead this soul again to the Virgin of Light, and again this soul gives the Virgin of Light the seals and the glory hymns, and the Virgin of Light and the seven other Virgins of the Light all try this soul, to find their signs in her, their seals, their baptisms, their unctions. And the Virgin of Light seals this soul, and the Receivers of Light baptize this soul to give her spiritual unction. And each of the Virgins of Light seals her with her seal, and again the Receivers ascend to the great Sabaoth the Good, who is near the Gate of Life, in the place of those at the right He whom one called the Father, and this soul gives Him the glory of her praises, of her seals, and of the passwords, and the great Sabaoth seals her with His seals, and the soul gives her knowledge and the glory of praises, and of seals to all the place at the right. All seal her with their seals, and Melchizedec, the great Receiver of Light, who lives in the place of those who are at the right, and all the Receivers of Melchizedec seal this soul, and Melchizedec leads her into the Treasury of Light. She gives glory, honor and glorification of hymns, with the seals of all the places of light. And all those of the places of light and all

those of the Treasury of Light seal her with their seals, and she goes into the place of her inheritance.

He then who will receive the word only of this mystery which I have told you, when he has gone out of the material body of the archrons, when the Tranquilizing Receivers have come to untie the material body from the matter of the eons, (for the Tranquilizing Receivers are those who detach each soul which goes out of the body,) when the Tranquilizing Receivers have detached the soul which has received this one and ineffable mystery, the one which I just told you, when it is detached from the body of matter, it will become a great ray of light in the midst of these Receivers, and the Receivers will fear greatly in the presence of the light of this soul. They will swoon, they will fall, they will immediately cease to act, for fear of the great ray of light, and the Receivers can not touch her, and will not know which is the road where she will go, for she has become a great ray of light, that she may go on high, and no thing (no virtue) can keep her back in any degree, or even approach her, but she will pass across all the places of the emanations of light, and she will not give the sentence, and she will not give the password at all, and she will not give any symbol for none of the virtues of the archons, none of the virtues of the emanations of light can approach this soul. But all the places of the archrons, and all the places of the emanations of light, each of them will sing a hymn in their place filled with fear in the presence of the light of the ray which will clothe this soul until she has crossed all the places, and has gone to the place of inheritance of the mystery that she has received, and it is the mystery of this unequalled and ineffable being that she is united to her fellows.

Explanation on the Subject of the Receivers.

And this is the manner in which the angels of light visit a brother of good conduct, as has been revealed many times by our Lord. If it is a good man who is dead, three angels come to him, according to the kind of the conduct of the one who is dead. If he is elevated in his actions, correspondingly elevat-

ed and glorious angels are sent to him to conduct him to God. If he is little in his virtues, proportionately inferior angels are sent him. At the moment when the man is on the point of giving up his soul, one of the angels stands near his head, another at his feet, under the form of men, who anoint him with their own hands until the soul goes out of the body, and the other unfolds a great spiritual vestment to clothe him with its glory.

Should it be the soul of a holy man, it is found beautiful in form and white as snow.

And when the soul has gone out of the body into the vestment, the angels take the two ends of the garment, one behind, the other at the front, just as men raise a body from earth, and the other angel sings, going before, in a tongue which no man knows, not even those who saw the vision, who are our Fathers Pakome and Theodore; for they do not know that which the angels sing, but they hear the angel singing and saying "Alleluia."

It is thus they go with the soul into the air, towards the east, going not as men by their feet, but gliding on their way like flowing water, because they are spirits. They go with the soul towards the heights, that it may see the limits of the inhabited world from one extremity to another, that it may see all creation, and that it may give glory to God who has created it. After that they show it the place of its repose, according to the order of the Lord, in order that after she is gone to the place of her rest on account of the good works that she has done. She should know, also, the punishments from which she has been saved, that she may bless still more the Lord, who has saved her from all these sufferings by the grace of our Lord Jesus the Christ.

THE DIVINE MYSTERY. 145

CHAPTER IV.

Jesus and Initiation.

Where then, O Egypt,
Are the diviners and the horoscopes,
And those who incant by the earth,
And those who incant by the entrails?
May they teach you henceforth the works
Which the Lord God of Sabaoth will do.

Then the spirit which was in Isaiah, the prophet, has so prophesied before Thy coming, and has prophesied of Thee that Thou wilt take away the spirit of the archons, and that Thou wilt change their sphere and their destiny that they may know nothing henceforth.

That is why the spirit said: "You will know nothing which the Lord God of Sabaoth (Seigneur Sabaoth) will do." That is to say, none of the archons knows what Thou wilt do from this time forth; that is to say, of Egypt, for it is to it that the prophesy relates. The spirit of prophesy (vertu) which was in the prophet Isaiah prophesied concerning Thee in the former time, saying: "From this time forth thou shalt not know what the Lord of Sabaoth will do," because of the virtue which you have received from the good Lord Sabaoth, he who is on the right hand, the virtue which to-day forms thy physical body.

That is why Thou hast said to us, O my Lord Jesus: "He that hath ears to hear, let him hear." For Thou knowest him whose heart is eager to enter into the kingdom of heaven.

Creation of Christianity.

Involution of the celestial principles which come to constitute terrestrial individualities who are to create Christianity.

Man possesses in himself the principle for his own ascent (or regeneration.) Let him unite, by any means whatever, his immortal spirit to the celestial essence which accompanies him during his life in the physical body, and he becomes a participant in the first mystery, as Valentine says; "a Saint" says

THE DIVINE MYSTERY.

Catholicism; "a Chrestos" or "Christos" say elementary schools of Initiation; "He will be born no more; he will partake of Nirvana," say the Oriental and Brahmanical schools.

Now, here is a formidable snare, about which it is important to be warned.

Each evolution supposes one or two involutions. Every man who becomes God necessitates a God who becomes man, as the changes of food in the intestines necessitates the descent of two forces of a higher origin—blood and nervous forces.

It is through a mistake concerning this remark about the stream of sacrifice and love, which precedes the hard path of Initiation and of evolution of the human soul, that the naturalist initiations of the Orient have led many of their adepts to believe that "the state of Christ" was a plane of psychic existence, which every man could reach, and which did not necessitate the constant effert of the celestial Christ principle, capable alone by His involution to lead evolved souls back to Himself.

Just as a comet, true blood-drop of the Universe, as Michel de Figanieres has said, comes at certain intervals, to give again to the solar families life from the higher centers, so, likewise, besides the constant current of Divine Involution and evolution of human souls, it if necessary at certain times that there be a great Divine descent, followed by a great ascent of human souls to give God the occasion of showing His absolute Love in advance of the time for the re-integration of the whole of humanity.

Not to see existence as celestial individuality from the Virgin of Light, from Christ, and from other principles, is to stop on the way; to stay on the mental plane, which leads to materialistic pantheism; to shut the eyes voluntarily to the existence of the celestial plane, which the virtues of the heart, love and prayer reach more rapidly than mental forces, criticism and reason.

To have united celestial love manifested by grace and redemption to the love of man for Heaven, manifested by prayer and sacrifice, that is the whole secret of the power of the Christians; of the white race (men?) illuminated by Christ, who are called to rule the whole earth on the day when they shall

replace the law of violence by the law of tolerance and love.

Valentine goes on to describe to us the descent of the heavenly principles which come to prepare safety for the white race by establishing Christianity. There is a whole chapter of this secret history of the Savior, reserved in the first century for the most advanced Initiations.

Incarnation of Jesus.

After that it happened then that, in the order of the First Mystery, I looked again down toward the world of humanity. I found Mary, her whom they call my mother according to the material body. I spoke to her under the form of Gabriel, and when she looked up on high towards me, I threw into her the first essence which I had received from the hand of Barbillo; that is to say, the body I had worn on High, and in place of the soul I threw into her the virtue which I had received from the hand of the Great Sabaoth the Good, he who exists on the right.*

The Virgin Mary.

It is to the Virgin of Light that Mary, the mother of Jesus, came.

Thou, also, O Mary, thou, who hast taken form in Barbillo, according to matter, and thou hast taken a resemblance to the Virgins of Light according to light, thou, and the other Mary, most happy. Shadows have existed on account of thee, and yet from thee has come forth the physical body which I bear and which I have purified.

The following extract will present us a new and profound mystery:

Jesus, as a man, lived until the age of twelve years of terrestrial life. It was not until that age that His divine nature really took possession of His physical being.

---

*Thus, contrary to the ordinary constitution of human beings, all the principles constituting the personality of Christ came from the celestial plane. See first part of this work. In the man, the heavenly principle (which does not incarnate) alone comes from this plane.

THE DIVINE MYSTERY. 151

The adepts of the schools of naturalist initiation will see there the union of the lower and higher principles in order to constitute the Christ.

One would say that the Gnostic doctor had seen across the centuries the error to be shunned in this matter; for he takes care to describe with great detail, involution, the descent of each of the celestial principles which are materialized to constitute a human being.

The Incarnation of the Spirit of Jesus.

Mary then spoke, she said: "My Lord, concerning the word which your spirit has prophesied by David, 'Mercy and Truth are met together. Righteousness and Peace have kissed each other. Truth has flourished on the earth, and Justice has looked down from Heaven.' Thy spirit has prophesied this aforetime concerning Thyself?"

The Fire Mystery.

"When Thou wert small, before the spirit had descended on Thee, when Thou wert in the vineyard with Joseph, the spirit descended from the heights and came to me in my house, resembling Thee, and as I did not know him and thought it was Thou, he said to me, 'Where is Jesus, my brother, that I may meet Him?'

"And when he said that to me I was troubled and thought it was an apparition to try me. I took him and fastened him to the foot of the bed, which was in my house, until I had gone to find you in the field, Thee and Joseph, and when I found you in the veneyard, Joseph was busy putting the vine on its support. It happened that, having heard me tell this thing to Joseph, Thou understoodest the thing. Thou rejoicedst, and said: 'Where is he that I may see him? No, I will wait for him here.' And it happened that Joseph, having heard Thee say these words, was in trouble, and we went together, and entered into the house, and found the spirit attached to the bed, and we looked at Thee with him. We found that Thou resembled him. And he who was attached to the bed, unfastened himself and embraced Thee, he kissed Thee, and Thou also kissed him. *You became one and the same person.*"

THE DIVINE MYSTERY. 153

"Here is the explanation of that matter. Pity is the spirit which comes from the heights through the first mystery. Take pity on the human race. He sent his spirit to pardon the sins of the whole world that men might receive the mystery; that they might inherit the Kingdom of Light. Truth, also, is the principle which abides in me, come from Barbillo. It has become thy physical body, and has acted as herald in place of truth (pity). Justice is thy spirit which has led all mysteries from above to give them to the human race. Peace, also, is the principle which has lived in thy physical body according to the world. That Body which has baptized the human race to make it a stranger to sin and keep it in peace with thy spirit, that they may be in peace with the emanations of Light; that is to say, that Justice and Peace may kiss each other. And, according to what has been told, Truth has flourished on earth. Truth is thy physical body, which has grown in me in the world of men. And, yet more, according to what has been written, Justice has bloomed outside of Heaven, which will give the mysteries of Light to the human race, and men will become just; they will be good; they will inherit the Kingdom of Light."

The Twelve Apostles.

Like the souls of Christ and Mary, the souls of the twelve Apostles did not come from the world of the archons, but really from the celestial (Fire) plane, as the following extract affirms:

"Rejoice, then, be full of joy, for when I came into the world from the beginning I led with me twelve powers, as I have told you from the beginning. I received them from the hands of the twelve Saviors of the Treasury of Light, according to the order of the first mystery. These powers, then, have I thrown into my mother, on my coming into the world, and it is they which are now in your bodies.

"And the twelve virtues of the twelve Saviors (or deliverers) of the Treasury of Light, which I have received from the hands of the twelve gods of the midst, I have thrown them into the sphere of the archons, and the gods of the archons with their liturges thought that they were the souls of the archons, and

the liturges led them; I fastened them in the bodies of your mothers, and, when your time had been accomplished, you were put into the world without having the souls of archons."

Role of the Apostles.

"In truth, in truth I say unto you this: I will make you perfect in all the pleromas, from the mysteries of the interior to the mysteries or the exterior. I will fill you with the spirit so that you will be called spiritual (pneumatique), perfect in all the pleromas. And, indeed, indeed, I say unto you, I will give unto you all the mysteries of all the places of my Father, and of all the places of the first mystery, that he whom you lead on earth will be led into the light on high, and him whom you reject on the earth will be rejected in the kingdom of my Father in Heaven."

All the manifestations which preside at the birth of Christianity are persons from the celestial (Fire) plane. It is by a sublime divine involution that the evolution of souls are made possible. This is the peculiar and high character of Christianity, the origin of its most profound mysteries. Each human race may be the object of a special Messianism; but at each new Messianism the new race presents itself on a more elevated plane of the evolutionary spiral.

The white race is that which has been called forth by the last Divine manifestation. It is not just, even after the laws of evolution, time and space, that this manifestation should have been more elevated than the preceding ones, and that it should have necessitated an involution of an order correspondingly elevated.

We offer these ideas as a subject of meditation to those who really know analogical methods and the mysterious laws which it translates.

The Two Clothings or Vestments.

The first has in it the whole glory of all the names of all mysteries and of all the emanations of the hierarchies of the places of the Ineffable.

And the second vestment has in it the glory of the names of all the mysteries and of all the emanations which exist in the

hierarchies of the two places of the first mystery.

And this vestment, which we have just described, is in itself the glory of the name of the mystery of the Commandant, or Chief, which is the first order, and the mystery of the five gulfs, and the mystery of the great ambassador of the Ineffable, who is this great Light, and the mystery of the five pro "hegonomeres," who are the five parastates (the thickened sides of a building, resembling columns—the sides of a porch).

We have been present at the birth of a great period.

As always, law is the same, and secondary periods will have their birth.

Indeed, each human life reproduces the two falls and the two ways of possible safety. The first fall is that of a soul into the body of flesh. The second, always avoided, is the entire possession of the soul by its passions and its progressive "deundation."

The first way of escape is in taking the soul away from the attractions of the flesh by holiness of life and absolute charity. The second way, complimentary to this, is the creation of the whole being by the fusion of two kindred souls. This is, in humanity, the image of the redemption made by Christ, and it is a very important key of the Way, the Truth and the Life.

CHAPTER V.

The Key To the Salvation of the Incarnate Soul; or Evangelical Initiation.

Man is on earth for the purpose of *reuniting his lower elements to his Divine elements*, and that can only be done by *Initiation*, which transforms the corporal into the spiritual.

The soul which has not been Initiated must come back into a body which will lead it to the way of Initiation.

These are important truths, and those of which one will find the rudiments in the inferior schools of the Orient, who believe, besides, that they may attain by this teaching all truth. It is not so at all.

If the soul is to be saved and escape the wheel of re-birth

must be Initiated, it is right to declare that Christ has multiplied the ways of this Initiation.

Besides Initiation, strictly personal, and based on suffering and sacrifice, Jesus comes, thanks to the Gospel, to show many ways of escape adaptable to all kinds of human beings. Furthermore, He comes to affirm that the Initiate—the "saint" (as the Christians say) the spirit (pneumatique), or the Apostle— has the right to remit sins and to Initiate directly those whom he considers susceptible of receiving this grace.

And more, Valentine reveals to us the connection between the Old and New Testament, in the course of the explanations which Jesus gives to His Disciples, who ask Him:

It is then a little esotericism of the Gospel which that portion of "Pistis Sophia," with which we are to occupy ourselves, will reveal to us?

Work of Jesus.

That is why I said to you formerly, "Seek that ye may find."

I have then said to you, "You shall search for the mysteries of light, those which purify the material body, and they will make you pure, very pure Light."

In truth, I tell you the race of humanity is physical. I am exhausted. I have brought to them all the mysteries of Light in order to purify them, for they are the dregs of all the matter of their matter, for otherwise no soul of the entire race of humanity would be saved or could inherit the Kingdom of Light if I had not carried to them the purifying mysteries.

For the emanations of Light have no need of the mystery, for they are pure; but the human race has need of purification, because all men are the dregs of matter. That is why I have said of old, "Those who are well need no physician but those who are sick." That is to say, those of the Light have no need of the mysteries, because they are pure Lights, but the human race it had need of them because they are corporal dregs.

Therefore announce to all the human race, saying: "Cease not to seek night and day until you have found the purifying mysteries; and say to the race humanity, give up the entire

world and all that it contains, for he who buys and sells this world, he who eats and drinks of its abundance, who lives in all its success and in all its relations, gathers for himself other material things from its matter; for this world, all that belongs to it, all its relations, are very corporal dregs, and try all concerning its purity.

For it is for sinners that I have brought the mysteries into the world, that I may pardon all their sins which they have committed since its beginning.

That is why I have said unto you aforetime, "I am not come to initiate the just." Now, then, I have brought the mysteries that sins may be pardoned to all men that they may come to the Kingdom of Light, for the mysteries are the gift of the first mystery, that it may blot out the sins and the iniquities of all sinners.

"*I Am Come To Bring Division.*"

Key to Baptism.

On the subject, then, of the word on the remission of sins, that you have given us formerly in a parable, saying, "I am come to bring fire on the earth, and what should I wish except that it may be lighted?" As you have explained it clearly in saying, "There is a baptism with which it is necessary that I should be baptised, and how shall I be kept back until it is accomplished? Do you think I am come to bring peace on the earth? No; but I am come to bring a division, for from henceforth five shall be in a house, three shall be divided against two, and two against three."

That, my Lord, is what you have said clearly, the word that you have spoken, "I have come to bring fire on the earth, and what do I wish if not that it be lighted?"

That is to say, my Lord, that you have brought to the world the mysteries of baptism, and what do you wish if not that it devours all the sins of soul, that it purifies them all?

And, then, you have clearly defined it, saying, "I have a baptism in which I must be baptised, and how shall I be strengthened until it be accomplished?"

That is to say, that you will not remain in the world until these

baptisms are accomplished; till they have purified the souls. And, again, the word that you have spoken formerly, "You think that I have come to bring peace on earth. No; but rather division, for from henceforth there shall be five in one house divided; three against two, and two against three." That is to say, that the mystery of baptism that you have brought into the world has made a division in the bodies of the world, or the body, because the Spirit of Spiritual Imitation, the body and Destiny, it has separated them on one side, and the soul, also, with the essence, has separated on the other side; that is to say, three is against two, and two against three.

First Sense.

We must give to the king that which belongs to the king, and give to God that which is God's. That is to say, when the soul has received the mystery she gives the apology (password) to all the archons and the palace of King Adamas. She gives honor and glory to all those of the place of Light and the Word; that is to say, "It has shone." When you saw that it was of silver and of brass, that is the type of that in which is the virtue of the Light; that is to say, the choice silver, and that which is in the Spirit of the Spiritual Imitation; that is to say, the corporal brass. There is, my Lord, the First Sense.

Second Sense.

The Second Sense, also, that Thou hast finished telling us concerning the soul who has received the mysteries; that is to say, a Savior. When she has gone to the place of the archons of the way of the midst, then they go before her in great fear, and the soul gives to them the mystery of the fear, and she fears before her and puts destiny in her place, and she gives the defence (password) and the seals to each of the archons who are on the way, and she gives honor, glory and glorification of the seals and of the hymns to all those of the place of Light.

Concerning this saying, my Lord, Thou hast told us formerly by the mouth of Paul, our Brother. "Give tribute to those who collect tribute, give fear to those who are worthy of fear, give honor to those who are worthy of honor, give glorification to him who is worthy of glorification, and give nothing to any-

one against you; that is to say, who has received the mysteries gives the defence in all places. That is, my Lord, the second meaning.

Third Sense.

As to the Third Sense, it is on the Word that Thou hast spoken to us formerly. The Spirit of Spiritual Imitation is the enemy of the soul, so that it causes it to commit all sins and (give itself to) all passions, and it takes it into all torments, on account of all the sins which it has made it commit. In a word, it is the enemy of the soul in every way. On the subject of the Word which Thou hast spoken to us formerly, that is: "The enemies of the men are they of their own househould;" that is to say, the household of the soul are the Spirits of Spiritual Imitation and Destiny, who are the enemies of the soul in all time, who make it commit all sins and iniquities. That is, my Lord, the Third Sense.

Fourth Sense.

As to the Fourth Sense, it is on the subject of the saying that Thou hast spoken to us: "When the soul has gone out of the body, and it goes in the way with the Spirit of Spiritual Imitation." If it does not find the mystery of the dissolution of all the bonds and the seals, those which bind the Spirit of Spiritual Imitation it may cease to fight her (the soul). If, then, she does not find them at all, the Spirit of Spiritual Imitation introduces to the Virgin of Light, who is the judge; that is to say, the Virgin of Light tries the soul in order to find whether she has sinned, and to find, also, whether she has with her the mysteries of Light, and she gives her to one of the Receivers, and her receiver leads her and throws her into the body, and she does not go out of the change of the body until she has paid the uttermost sheckel. Concerning this word, then, my Lord, Thou hast spoken to us formerly, "Agree with thine adversary quickly, while thou art in the way with him, for fear thine enemy wilt deliver thee to the judge; that the judge deliver thee to the attendants; that the attendants throw thee into prison, that thou go not thence till thou hast paid the last mite." That is why the word has been clearly spoken: "Every soul that goes

out of the body goes on the way with the Spirit of Spiritual Imitation, and that it does not find the mystery of dissolving all the seals and all the bonds that it may detach the Spirit of Spiritual Imitation which is attached to her, well, this soul who has not received the mystery in Light, who has not found the mystery of dissolution of the Spirit of Spiritual Imitation which is attached to her, if, then, she has not found it, the Spirit of Spiritual Imitation introduces this soul to the presence of the Virgin of Light, who is the judge, will deliver this soul to the hands of one of the Receivers, and the Receiver throws her into the sphere of the Eons. She goes not forth from the changings of the body, and she does not give the uttermost farthings which belongs to her. That, my Lord, is the Fourth Sense.

CHAPTER VI.

The Initiates On Earth.

Is it necessary to pardon the Initiate who sins then corrects himself at each degree of initiation?

Not only pardon him until seven times, but, in truth, pardon him until seven times a multitude of times. Give him at each time the mysteries from the beginning; those which are in the first place even from the outer. Perhaps you will gain the soul of that brother so that he may inherit the kingdom of Light.

That is why, when you have asked me formerly, saying: "If our brother sin against us, dost Thou wish we should pardon him till seven times?" I said to you: "Not only until seven times, but until seventy times seven." Now, then, pardon him innumerable times. Give him every time the outer mysteries, those which are in the first part. Indeed, I say unto you this: "He who will test a single soul, and save it besides the Light which he has in the kingdom of Light, he will receive another glory for the soul he has saved, and he who saves many souls, beyond the glory which he has in glory will receive many other glories for the souls which he saves.

That is on account of the souls of men, of the kind of which

you have spoken before in a parable: "If thy brother sin against thee forgive him. If he harkens to thee, thou wilt gain the brother. If he does not harken unto thee, take with thee another brother. If he does not listen to thee then, nor to this other brother, lead him to the assembly. If he does not listen to these others, let him be to us as a transgressor and an outcast.

And if he is not worthy of the first mystery, give him the second; and if he is not worthy of the second, give him successively the third. That is what the assembly means; and if he is not worthy in the third mystery, let him be for you an outcast and a transgressor.

And the word which I said unto you formerly: "Every word will be established before two or three witnesses," means that these three mysteries witness against his last repentance; and, in truth, I say unto you, if this man repents, there is no mystery which pardons his sins and receives his repentance. There is no means whatever of hearing him in any mystery whatever, unless it may be by the first mystery of the first mystery and mysteries of that Ineffable. Those only will receive the repentance of that man and will pardon his sins; for these mysteries are all-pitiful and merciful, pardoning at all times.

It is on account of men of this sort (Initiates through hyprocrisy, who deride the mysteries after having received them) that I have spoken to you formerly in a parable saying: "Into whatsoever house ye enter, first say peace be unto you, and if they are worthy let your peace repose on them; and if they are not worthy, let your peace return to you."

Words of Jesus.

Concerning Repentance.

Happy is every man who abases himself, for it is on him that they will have pity.

He whose spirit is wise, him will I not hinder at all; but I will encourage him to speak the truth that has incited him. Whoever will be filled with the Spirit of Light, that he may go and speak the explanation of what I say, no one will hinder from speaking. Where your treasure is there will your heart be

THE DIVINE MYSTERY.

also. That is to say, the place where each has received the mystery, there he will stay.

I am the knowledge of the Pleroma. He who believes on a prophet will receive the reward of a prophet, and he who believes on a just person will receive the reward of a just person.

I pardon, and I will pardon; and it is for that that the first mystery has sent me, that I may pardon the sins of all the world.

And you yourselves try him (the recipient in good faith) in order to know of what mystery he is worthy, and conceal nothing from him; for if you conceal anything from him, you will be subject to a great judgment.

Indeed, indeed, I say to you not only will I reveal all things to you which you ask, but now I will tell you things concerning which you do not think of asking; those which have not come to the heart of man, all those of the other Gods which are in the heart of man not to know.

CHAPTER VII.

The Way of Initiation.

Whoever has trouble, and suffers under his burden, come to me, and I will comfort you, for my burden is light and my yoke is easy.

The mystery (that of the Ineffable) is yours and his who will listen to you; renounce the world and all that is in it; renounce all bad thoughts and all cares of this Eon.

Whoever will give up the world and all that is in it, who will submit himself to Divinity, this mystery will be much easier for him than all the mysteries of the kingdom of Light.

Theurgy.

Now, then, O Mary, not only you, but all men who will accomplish the mystery of the resurrection of the dead, he who will cure demons, the sick of all sickness and, also, the blind, the lame, the crippled, the dumb and the deaf, as I have said to you formerly: He who will receive a mystery, and do it, if,

THE DIVINE MYSTERY. 173

then, he asks anything whatever, poverty or riches, feebleness or strength, sickness or a healthy body, as well as all cures of the body, with the resurrection of the dead, the healing of the lame, the blind, the deaf and mute, of all suffering; in a word, who accomplishes this mystery, if he asks all things of which I have just spoken, they will be given him cheerfully.

As to the mystery of raising the dead, of curing the sick, do not give it to any one and do not teach it, for this mystery is that of the archons and all its names. That is why you must not give it to any or teach it, until you have strengthened faith in all the world, so that when you enter into cities or countries and they do not receive you, nor believe in you, nor obey your word, you will raise there the dead in those places, cure the lame, the blind, different sicknesses in those places; and, by all these means, they will believe in you; they will believe that you preach the God of the Pleroma, and they will increase faith in every word coming from you. That is why I have given you this mystery, until you have established on the whole world.

In truth, in truth, I tell you, you will be the first in the kingdom of the heavens, before all the Invisible ones and all the Gods, except the archons who are in the thirteenth Eon and those who are in the twelfth Eon; and not only you, but also whoever will do my mysteries.

When He had said that, He said to them: "Do you understand the way in which I speak to you?" Mary burst forth again and said: "Yes, my Lord, it is that which you have said to us formerly; that is, 'The last will be the first, and the first shall be the last.' The first were those who were created before us are the Invisible ones. It is they who were created before humanity; they and the gods and the archons; and the men who receive the mysteries will be before them in the kingdom of the heavens." Jesus said unto her: "Courage, Mary."

Thou hast said unto us formerly: "The first shall be last and the last shall be first;" that is to say, the last of the whole human race who will be the first in the kingdom of Light, according to the way of all who are in the place of the Light, it is they who will be the first.

CHAPTER VIII.

Total Re-Integration.

Now, then, in truth, I tell you this: When the number of perfect is complete and the Pleroma will rise, I will seat myself in the Treasury of Light, and you, also, will be seated on the twelve hierarchies of the twelve Saviors in the place of the heritage for each of them.

When He had said these things, He said: "Do you understand what I say?" Mary advanced again and said: "Lord, on this subject, you have spoken formerly in a parable, 'You have endured temptations with me. I will establish a kingdom for you, as my Father has established one for me, that you may eat, that you may drink, at my table in my kingdom, and you shall be seated on twelve thrones to judge the twelve tribes of Israel.'" He said unto her: "Courage, Mary."

And in the dissolution of the world, when the Pleroma will make its ascension, when shall have mounted the number of all perfect souls, then I shall be king in the midst of the Parastate.

Then all those men who have received the mystery in the Ineffable will be co-regent with me. They will be seated at my right and at my left in my kingdom. And, in truth, I say these men are myself and myself are these men. That is why I said to you aforetime, "You will be seated at my right and at my left in my kingdom, and you will reign with me."

On these points, the revelations collected by Valentine are not as interesting as the entirely new developments which he has given us on the agents charged with presiding at the earthly birth and death whom he calls Receivers, who are themselves qualified according to their dadius of action. We can say without hesitation that these instructions given on spiritual beings touch on the most profound mysteries of the temples of Initiation of antiquity, and if one knows that the Virgin of Light, the Celestial Father (Iao), the Grand Receiver Melchizedec, are teachings reserved to the High Kabbala one will account for the great light brought into the outer darkness by the Gnostic doctor.

THE DIVINE MYSTERY. 177

But it is not sufficient for him to describe to us the different ways which are offered to the soul after death. He insists further, and often on the truly Divine way, of the Virgin of Light which offers to sinning souls safety by reincarnation. The key of the mystery of birth is thus given from the second century of our era, at the same time as the key of the mysteries of death.

The Universal Spirit would lead the savages by that way to the road to Unity. Thus, also, does the Initiate act concerning all religions. He goes into the midst of the clergy, in the midst of the sects of materialism, and into the midst of the profane, enlightens them and directs them to the harbor of truth in which each of their habitual ways lead.

But he takes good care not to convert them by strategy, by force, or by gifts, to any particular religion, for it is the spirit itself of Christ, in permanent action on the earth, which will lead souls into the light, and that without severity and without violence.

We must, indeed, not forget that there are three stages of psychical development in each division of study, and the occultist is subject to this rule, like all other seekers, until he has penetrated into the plane of Unity by the spiritual way.

The first stage is obligatory for all. When one follows the way of the intellect is the rational stage. Facts only appeal to the mind which does not seek to know laws or principles, be they spiritists, magnetic or magic, it matters little, it is indispensible to establish the reason on the rock of experience. There is found the key of the physical sciences through the elementary Kabbala and the rudiments of Alchemy.

Many beginners imagine that all occultism stops there, and it is, indeed, there that every thing useful to teaching and diffusion of the elements of the occult is found.

It is a very curious thing that the human intelligence only arriving at this point after having attained self-government, and after having gotten rid of all teachings purely mystical, and without experimental base, imagines that it has come to the height of its development when it is only in its infancy. So

THE DIVINE MYSTERY.

those who think themselves liberated, minds free from prejudice and superstition, look with supreme disdain on brothers who have attained higher degrees, but who appear to them to have retrogressed and degenerated. It is a strange error of the mind and much more common than one would imagine.

For just as great courage has been necessary to rid oneself of old ideas and admit the truth of occultism with its consequences, so just as much or more courage is required to come out of the egotism of this first stage and to commence the development of the heart and the feelings, whereas only intellectual development was necessary to the first stage.

How can one begin again to read the "Initiation," (of Christ) the Gospels, the Buddhist books of morality; how to arrive at certitude concerning the facts of which they treat, facts as certain as the occult truths? How, in short, to open the moral being to prayer and to the influence from on high when one thinks himself "somebody," and when one has made himself center in the Universe?

There is one way to that. Humility, and return to the plan of universal communion, where the stone, the plant, and all the forms of the Soul of the world unite in the same united thanksgiving. Cease to think of yourself as any one; have the feeling before the immense Power from on High you are hardly anything; fraternize with your inferiors who suffer; go to the homes of the poor in heart, in mind, in body, and teach them to bless their trials, and to hate no more, and slowly, slowly your free reason, your proud Will will bow under its blessedness without losing anything of their qualities, and the life of the heart will wake in you.

Then facts will be effaced before the ideas which they reveal and which they translate. The divisions of religions and of sects disappear in universal love for sinners and for the weak; and the soul, intoxicated by ecstasy and by the Infinite, escapes little by little those terrestral things on which it is its duty to exercise its activity.

But the human being is complete only by the union of sister souls separated during physical incarnation, just as spiritual

Being is only born in man in all its splendor if by a new and great effort man accomplishes the union of the brain and heart, of Fact and of Law, in order to develop the unity of the principle.

This knowledge, illuminated by faith, and this faith strengthened by knowledge, one must devote to the evolution of the feeble and the oppressed, and action more than natural must now be the endeavor of him who aspires to the conscious sufferings of the third degree.

Always unknown, he must save even those who ridicule and insult him; he must guard them from harm and take it upon himself if necessary. And he never shows his real powers, or says that he is superior to the most ignorant or the most sinful of men; for he is in the plane where all superiority has disappeared before the necessity of entire devotion.

This is the way indicated in the Fraternity of Rose Cross; that is the way the Brotherhood, and it is the way which Jesus has revealed to those who wish to follow Him.

One never attains the Path of the Lords of Life and of Suffering in the astral body; only the spiritual is capable of reaching that.

But the student who attempts even the first of the three stages must have enough knowledge to respect the mystic, and enough courage to kill the warrior who fights in his heart of selfishnessness and pride.

Re-read the Repentances of Pistis Sophia, that lasting model for every being who wishes to unite the devotion of the heart to the knowledge of the brain; seek again for divine words even though brought to you by a Gnostic Doctor. Shun clerical despotism, whether it comes from a materialistic savant, this priest of nothingness, or from a sectarian who wishes to convert by severity, excommunication, or by force.

FINIS.

www.ingramcontent.com/pod-product-compliance
Lightning Source LLC
Chambersburg PA
CBHW031433150426
43191CB00006B/502